fast fresh &
fabulous

Janelle Bloom

Photography by Steve Brown

EBURY
PRESS

Contents

Fast fresh & fabulous has been in the making for about 8 years. I have always loved to cook, for myself, family and friends, and on a weekly basis I would add recipes I love to the **fast fresh & fabulous** folder on my computer.

I hope this book and my simple, no-fuss approach and detailed explanations in each and every recipe will inspire you to cook more often.

I was raised in the most loving and food-filled environment. My mum cooked every night of the week, baked treats for our school lunch boxes and when she wasn't in the kitchen, my adorable late grandmother was. Sometimes we were all in the kitchen: they were the best days of my life. When I close my eyes I can smell the lingering aroma of lamb roasting on a Sunday, schnitzel frying, cakes and bread baking and dumplings simmering, just to name a few. With these memories I was taught to share, be generous, smile and never take anything for granted.

My approach to food is simple. I believe good food should be a combination of **fast fresh & fabulous**. Fast either in preparation, cooking, shopping, cleaning or a combination of all four. To cook fresh, start with the very best ingredients you can afford; get to know your butcher, greengrocer and fishmonger and they will look after you. Limit the preservatives in your diet by using fresh ingredients — I believe this is as important, if not more, than worrying about the fat and sugar in our diets. Fabulous: well, all food should be fabulous, and homemade should be a part of everyone's regime.

Great memories often revolve around food with family and friends. Remember food is a sure-fire way to everyone's heart. I hope the next time you share your table or give something homemade to a friend, one of the recipes in this book takes centre place. Happy cooking!

 This book is dedicated to my mum, dad and sisters Sharon and Wendy.
Every day I wake up and thank my lucky stars we are a part of each other's lives.

Fast

Fast can have so many meanings. Sometimes (well, nearly always) there doesn't seem to be enough time to get dinner on the table, therefore ingredients need to be accessible, and the preparation and cooking need to be speedy. Other days there might be time to start the preparation during the day or even the night before, so when it's time for dinner all that's left to do is the cooking. The recipes that follow reflect both these scenarios without compromising on flavour, as well as keeping the equipment, shopping and washing-up to a minimum.

Lemon, basil and pea spaghetti

serves 4

400g spaghetti
1 cup frozen peas
2 tablespoons extra virgin olive oil
2 garlic cloves, crushed
1 red chilli, deseeded, finely chopped
1 large lemon, rind finely grated, juiced
1 tablespoon fresh thyme leaves
1/2 cup basil leaves, shredded
150g fresh ricotta cheese

1 Cook spaghetti in a large saucepan of boiling salted water until al dente, adding the peas to the pasta for the last 2 minutes of cooking.

2 Meanwhile, heat 2 teaspoons oil in a non-stick frying pan over medium heat, add the garlic and chilli and cook 1-2 minutes until aromatic. Remove from the heat; add lemon rind, 1/4 cup lemon juice, thyme and the remaining oil.

3 Drain the pasta and peas and return to the hot saucepan over low heat. Add the lemon mixture and basil, season with salt and pepper and toss over low heat until well combined.

4 Pile into bowls, crumble over the ricotta, season with pepper and drizzle with a little extra oil if desired. Serve.

Don't add oil to the water when cooking pasta. It coats the pasta, preventing the sauce from sticking to it when tossed together.

In all my recipes I use firm fresh ricotta... from the deli (supermarket or other), not pre-packaged, tub ricotta.

Lemon, basil and pea spaghetti

Lemongrass beef and cashew stir-fry

Lemongrass beef and cashew stir-fry

serves 4

600g beef fillet steak, trimmed
2 teaspoons sesame oil
1 stick lemongrass, white part only, finely chopped
2 garlic cloves, crushed
1/2 cup cashew nuts
1 1/2 tablespoons peanut oil
1 tablespoon fish sauce
1 tablespoon grated palm sugar
1/2 lime, juiced
150g snow peas, thinly sliced on diagonal
cooked jasmine rice or rice noodles, to serve

1 Thinly slice beef across the grain (this helps keep the meat tender as it cooks). Combine sesame oil, lemongrass and garlic in a bowl, add beef and stir to coat.

2 Place cashews in a cold wok over high heat. Stir-fry for 4 minutes until nuts are toasted. Remove to a plate. Wipe wok clean. Heat the wok over high heat until hot (don't add the oil until the wok is hot as the oil will burn before the wok is hot enough for cooking).

3 Add 2 teaspoons peanut oil and swirl to coat the wok. Add one quarter of the beef and stir-fry for 30 seconds until sealed. Remove to a clean bowl. Repeat with remaining peanut oil and beef in three batches (cooking meat in batches means the wok stays very hot, searing the meat, not stewing it).

4 Combine fish sauce, palm sugar and 1 tablespoon lime juice in a bowl. Return all the beef and any juices to the wok. Add fish sauce mixture, snow peas and cashews, and stir-fry 30 seconds. Serve over rice or noodles.

Peanut oil is best for cooking over high heat as it won't burn as quickly as other oils.

Tandoori chicken

serves 4

200g Greek-style yoghurt
$1/3$ cup tandoori paste
$1^1/2$ teaspoons salt
$1/2$ teaspoon chilli powder
2 teaspoons ground coriander
2 teaspoons ground cumin
1 teaspoon garam masala
3 large garlic cloves, crushed
2cm piece fresh ginger, peeled, grated
8 chicken thigh fillets, trimmed
warm naan bread and salad leaves, to serve

Apple and mint raita
1 Lebanese cucumber, peeled, halved lengthways
2 Granny Smith apples, peeled
1 cup Greek-style yoghurt
2 tablespoons chopped fresh mint

1 Combine the yoghurt, tandoori paste, salt, chilli powder, ground coriander and cumin, garam masala, garlic and ginger in a ceramic dish. Add the chicken and turn to coat. Cover and refrigerate 2 hours if time permits.

2 Preheat oven to 250°C no fan/250°C fan-forced. Place the well-coated chicken on a lightly greased rack inside a roasting pan. Cook for 18-20 minutes or until slightly charred and cooked through.

3 Meanwhile, for apple and mint raita, use a teaspoon to scrape the seeds from the cucumber halves. Coarsely grate cucumber and apple. Squeeze out excess moisture. Combine cucumber, apple, yoghurt and mint in a bowl, season with salt and pepper. Cover and refrigerate until ready to serve.

4 Serve tandoori chicken with apple and mint raita, naan bread and salad leaves.

Greek-style yoghurt is a must in the kitchen — not only does it taste better, but it won't split or curdle when cooked.

This is one of my favourite recipes. I love cooking it for dinner as the leftovers can double as lunch the next day. Wrap the chicken, raita and some salad leaves in pita bread — simply delicious!

Tandoori chicken

Prawn market salad with lime and palm sugar dressing

Prawn market salad with lime and palm sugar dressing

serves 6

2 large telegraph cucumbers
3 medium carrots, peeled
250g bean sprouts, trimmed
1/4 small red cabbage, shredded
1 cup fresh mint leaves
1.5kg cooked king prawns, peeled, deveined

Lime and palm sugar dressing
2 tablespoons extra light olive oil
5 limes, juiced ($2/3$ cup)
1/2 cup grated palm sugar
2 tablespoons water
2 tablespoons sweet chilli sauce
3 teaspoons fish sauce
2cm piece fresh ginger, finely grated

1 For the lime and palm sugar dressing, place all the ingredients in a screw-top jar and shake well to combine. Refrigerate until ready to serve.

2 Cut the cucumbers in half and use a teaspoon to scrape the seeds from the halves. Cut cucumbers and carrots into thin matchsticks and combine in a large bowl. Add bean sprouts, cabbage, mint, prawns and dressing, then toss until well combined. Serve.

Palm sugar comes from palm tree sap. You will find it in the Asian section of your supermarket or you can use brown sugar.

 After a long day filming (and way too much eating), I grab some prawns and seasonal vegetables on the way home and throw this together. It's light and healthy with a low GI carbohydrate. It's a great main but can also be served as a starter when entertaining.

Antipasto quiche

serves 6

2 sheets shortcrust pastry, partially thawed
$1/2$ small bunch silverbeet, leaves shredded
$1^1/2$ cups chopped antipasto (like semi-dried tomatoes,
   roasted capsicum, char-grilled eggplant, stuffed olives)
4 green onions, thinly sliced
3 eggs
$2/3$ cup thickened cream
$2/3$ cup milk
80g fresh ricotta cheese, crumbled

1 Use pastry to line the base and sides of 2.5cm-deep, 26cm (base)
fluted quiche pan. Trim excess pastry. Place into the freezer
for 10 minutes or until firm.

2 Preheat the oven and a flat tray to 200°C no fan/180°C fan-forced.
Place the quiche pan onto the hot tray and bake pastry case for
10-12 minutes or until light golden. Remove quiche pan from oven,
leaving the tray. Reduce the oven to 180°C no fan/170°C fan-forced.

3 Scatter the silverbeet on the hot pastry base. Top with the
antipasto and green onions. Beat eggs, cream and milk with a fork
until just combined (don't overbeat as this creates air bubbles in
the custard). Season with salt and pepper. Pour the filling over the
silverbeet, crumble over the ricotta. Bake for a further 20-25 minutes
or until set in centre. Serve warm or at room temperature.

Commercial pastry tends to shrink a little more than the
homemade variety. Use kitchen scissors to trim excess pastry
so it sits just a little above the edge of the pan to allow
for shrinkage.

Antipasto quiche

Cheat's lasagne

Cheat's lasagne

serves 6

1 tablespoon olive oil
1 small red onion, halved, thinly sliced
2 large garlic cloves, crushed
3 x 400g cans whole tomatoes, roughly chopped
1 teaspoon white sugar
1/2 cup basil leaves, roughly chopped
800g fresh tortellini (Ubaldi King Island beef brand)
250g mozzarella cheese, thickly sliced
small basil leaves and pepper, to serve (optional)

1 Preheat oven to 210°C no fan/200°C fan-forced. Lightly grease 5cm-deep, 22cm x 30cm (base) baking dish.

2 Heat the oil in a saucepan over medium-high heat. Add onion and garlic, cook 3 minutes or until onion is soft. Add tomatoes and sugar and bring to the boil. Cook, stirring occasionally, for 10 minutes until sauce thickens slightly. Stir in the basil and season with salt and pepper.

3 Meanwhile, cook pasta in a large saucepan of boiling salted water for 3 minutes. Drain and spoon into prepared dish. Spoon over tomato sauce and stir to coat tortellini.

4 Top with mozzarella, bake uncovered for 20 minutes until bubbling around the edges. Sprinkle with extra basil leaves and pepper if desired. Serve.

The easiest way to chop tomatoes is to leave them in the can and use kitchen scissors to snip them.

You are going to love this. It looks and tastes like you have spent hours in the kitchen when in fact it takes only minutes.

Sichuan pork with cucumber and radish salad

serves 4

1 red onion, roughly chopped
3cm piece fresh ginger, peeled, chopped
2 small red chillies, chopped
5 large garlic cloves
1 teaspoon Chinese five-spice powder
1/3 cup kecap manis
1 tablespoon vegetable oil
4 pork chops

Cucumber and radish salad
2 Lebanese cucumbers, peeled, halved
6 red radishes, thinly sliced
100g baby rocket leaves
1/4 cup Greek-style yoghurt
1 tablespoon caster sugar
1 lime, juiced
1 tablespoon fish sauce

1 Combine the onion, ginger, chilli, garlic, five spice, kecap manis
and oil in a small food processor or mortar. Process or pound until
well combined. Spoon into a ceramic dish. Add pork and turn to coat
both sides. Cover and refrigerate for a minimum 30 minutes or
overnight if time permits.

2 For the cucumber and radish salad, use a teaspoon to scrape the
seeds from the cucumber halves. Thinly slice cucumbers and combine in
a bowl with radish and rocket. Combine yoghurt, sugar, 2 tablespoons
lime juice and fish sauce, then spoon over the salad and toss gently
to combine.

3 Preheat a barbecue plate on high until hot. Reduce heat to medium,
add pork and cook for 4 minutes each side or until just cooked
through. Spoon salad onto plates and serve with pork.

Peel any leftover ginger and store in a jar covered with sherry. It will keep for months in the fridge.

Sichuan pork with cucumber and radish salad

Spinach and two-cheese pizza

Spinach and two-cheese pizza

serves 4

1 quantity quick mix pizza dough (see page 224)
$2/3$ cup tomato passata sauce (see page 222)
100g baby spinach leaves
100g feta cheese
100g fresh ricotta cheese
$1/2$ cup roasted hazelnuts, roughly chopped
extra virgin olive oil

1 Preheat oven and two flat baking trays to 220°C no fan/200°C fan-forced. Cut pizza dough in half. Roll each piece out to a 22cm x 34cm rectangle (or oval). Place each onto a sheet of baking paper. Spread each base with 2 tablespoons tomato passata sauce. Slide onto hot trays and bake for 6-8 minutes, swap trays over and bake a further 4-5 minutes or until light golden. Remove from the oven.

2 Spread the remaining tomato passata sauce over pizzas, top with spinach. Crumble feta and ricotta over the spinach and sprinkle with hazelnuts. Bake a further 4-5 minutes until cheese is slightly melted. Season with salt and pepper, drizzle with olive oil. Serve.

You can buy two large (about 300g each) pizza bases instead.

 Commercial pizza does not compare with homemade. You can have this made and on the table more quickly than ordering in. It's helathier and much cheaper too.

Salt and pepper squid

serves 4

600g small cleaned squid tubes
4 garlic cloves, crushed
1 bunch dill, finely chopped
1/3 cup fish sauce
1 tablespoon grated palm sugar
2 teaspoons ground black pepper
vegetable oil, for deep frying
1/3 cup rice flour
1/3 cup cornflour
lime wedges and wild rocket, to serve

Lime salt and pepper mix
1 tablespoon black peppercorns
2 limes, rind grated
1 tablespoon salt flakes

1 For the lime salt and pepper mix, use a mortar and pestle to pound the peppercorns until roughly crushed. Add lime rind and salt and pound until well combined.

2 Cut squid in half. Using a sharp knife score the inside in a fine criss-cross pattern. Cut squid into 6cm pieces. Combine garlic, dill, fish sauce, palm sugar and pepper in a ceramic or glass bowl. Add squid and mix until well combined. Cover. Refrigerate for up to 2 hours, if time permits.

3 Preheat oven to 160°C no fan/150°C fan-forced. Pour oil into a heavy-based saucepan or wok until one-third full. Heat over medium-high heat until hot.

4 Combine the rice flour and cornflour in a bowl. Drain the squid and coat well in flour mixture. Deep-fry squid, in batches, for 2-3 minutes or until light golden. Use a slotted spoon to transfer squid to a wire rack. Keep warm on the rack in the oven while cooking remaining squid. Sprinkle with lime salt and pepper mix. Serve with lime wedges and wild rocket.

To check if the oil is hot enough, insert the handle of a wooden spoon into the oil. Small bubbles should appear in the area surrounding the handle. And remember to cook the squid in small batches. That way the oil retains its temperature and the squid absorbs a minimal amount of oil during cooking.

Salt and pepper squid

Agnolotti with roasted pumpkin and parmesan wafers

Agnolotti with roasted pumpkin and parmesan wafers

serves 4

750g butternut pumpkin, cut into 2cm cubes
1 tablespoon olive oil
625g packet fresh ricotta and spinach agnolotti pasta
90g butter, melted
1/2 teaspoon ground nutmeg
2/3 cup walnuts, roughly chopped
1/4 cup chopped fresh chives
2 tablespoons flat-leaf parsley leaves, roughly chopped

Parmesan wafers
1 cup finely grated parmesan cheese
1 teaspoon plain flour

Grate the parmesan just before cooking, or it will lose moisture and won't melt properly.

1 Preheat oven to 220°C no fan/200°C fan-forced. Line a baking tray with baking paper.

2 For the parmesan wafers, combine the parmesan and flour in a bowl, then season with salt and pepper. Sprinkle the mixture evenly over the tray. Bake 8-10 minutes or until light golden. Remove and allow to cool. Break into pieces. Increase oven to 230°C no fan/230°C fan-forced.

3 Place pumpkin on another lined baking tray. Drizzle with olive oil, season with salt and pepper. Roast for 15 minutes or until golden and tender.

4 Meanwhile, cook pasta in a large saucepan of boiling salted water, until al dente.

5 Heat butter in a frying pan over medium heat for 3 minutes or until golden, remove from heat and stir in the nutmeg and walnuts.

6 Drain pasta, reserving 2 tablespoons of the cooking water. Return pasta and reserved water to the hot saucepan. Add the pumpkin, walnut mixture, chives and parsley, then season with salt and pepper. Toss over low heat until well combined. Pile into bowls, sprinkle with parmesan wafers and serve.

Mustard, lemon and rosemary chicken

serves 4

$^1/_3$ cup Dijon mustard
$^1/_4$ cup olive oil
$^1/_4$ cup rosemary leaves, roughly chopped
$^1/_4$ cup flat-leaf parsley leaves, roughly chopped
3 garlic cloves, crushed
2 lemons, rind finely grated, juiced
2 x 1kg chickens, halved, backbones removed

1 Combine mustard, oil, rosemary, parsley, garlic, lemon rind and $^1/_2$ cup lemon juice in a jug. Whisk until well combined. Pour into a large ceramic dish.

2 Season chickens with salt and pepper. Place chickens in the marinade and turn to coat. Cover and refrigerate 2 hours or overnight if time permits.

3 Preheat oven to 200°C no fan/190°C fan-forced. Place chicken pieces on a roasting rack over a lined baking tray, then spoon over the marinade. Roast for 1 hour or until golden and cooked through. Serve with twice-fried chips (see page 229) and lemon-scented broccoli (see page 244).

Ask your butcher to do this for you if you don't have good kitchen scissors.

I love this dish. You can prepare and refrigerate it the night before, then put it straight into the oven to roast an hour before you want to eat it. You'll know when it's ready — the house will be filled with a sensational aroma.

Mustard, lemon and rosemary chicken

Barbecued lamb with bean, asparagus and pine nut salad

Barbecued lamb with bean, asparagus and pine nut salad

serves 4

Though lamb cutlets are pricey, I love them and spoil myself with them often.

12 lamb cutlets
1 tablespoon fresh thyme leaves
2 lemons, thinly sliced
extra virgin olive oil
300g baby beans
1 bunch asparagus, trimmed
1/2 cup semi-dried tomatoes
2 tablespoons toasted pine nuts

1 Place lamb on an oven tray, sprinkle both sides with thyme leaves and season with salt and pepper. Top with lemon slices and drizzle with oil.

2 Place washed beans and asparagus in a plastic bag and twist the top to secure. Microwave on High/100% for 1-2 minutes until bright green, or alternatively, blanch in boiling salted water. Drain well and pat dry with paper towel.

3 Preheat a barbecue plate or frying pan over medium-high heat. Add beans and asparagus, drizzle with a little oil and barbecue for 1-2 minutes or until tender. Transfer to a plate, then add semi-dried tomatoes and pine nuts.

4 Barbecue lamb for 3-4 minutes each side for medium or until cooked to your liking. Barbecue lemon slices 1-2 minutes each side until charred.

5 Place lamb and lemon over the beans and asparagus, drizzle with a little oil and serve.

Icky sticky ribs

serves 4

4 racks pork spare ribs
3/4 cup barbecue sauce
3/4 cup tomato sauce
2 tablespoons hoisin sauce
1/4 cup golden syrup
1-2 tablespoons hot chilli sauce
2 garlic cloves, crushed

1 Preheat oven to 180°C no fan/180°C fan-forced. Cover the base of a roasting pan with water. Place ribs in a single layer (slightly overlapping, if necessary) on a wire rack inside the pan. Cover tightly with foil. Bake for 1 hour. Remove from the oven, uncover and allow the ribs to cool completely.

2 Combine the barbecue sauce, tomato sauce, hoisin sauce, golden syrup, chilli and garlic and use two-thirds to spread all over the ribs. Cover and refrigerate overnight if time permits. Cover the remaining sauce and set aside until ready to serve.

3 Preheat a barbecue flat plate on medium heat until hot. Barbecue the ribs for 5-8 minutes each side until they are golden and warmed through. Remove to a tray and brush with remaining sauce. Serve with pink grapefruit and avocado salad (see page 73).

 Ribs are a winner every time they are served. I learnt this great technique of pre-cooking and marinating them from a very generous friend, Naomi. It means you can prepare ahead and the cooking time is only minutes.

Icky sticky ribs

Green chicken curry

Green chicken curry

serves 4

700g chicken thigh fillets, trimmed
1¹/₂ tablespoons vegetable oil
1 red onion, cut into thin wedges
2-3 tablespoons green curry paste
400ml can coconut milk (Ayam brand)
1 lime, juiced
3 teaspoons fish sauce
1 tablespoon grated palm sugar
150g baby spinach leaves
50g bean sprouts, trimmed
steamed jasmine rice, to serve
bean sprouts and coriander leaves, to serve (optional)

1 Thinly slice the chicken across the grain. Heat a wok over high heat until hot. Add 1 teaspoon oil and swirl to coat the wok. Add one-quarter of the chicken. Stir-fry for 1-2 minutes or until golden. Remove to a plate. Repeat with oil and remaining chicken in three batches.

2 Reduce heat to medium-high. Add remaining oil and onion to the wok, stir-fry for 1-2 minutes or until onion softens slightly. Add curry paste and cook, stirring, for 20-30 seconds or until aromatic.

3 Add the thick top layer of the coconut milk and cook for 1 minute or until it splits (this is known as cracking the milk), then add the remaining coconut milk. Bring to a gentle boil. Reduce heat to low and return the chicken and juices to the wok. Simmer for 5-10 minutes or until chicken is cooked through.

4 Combine 2 tablespoons lime juice, fish sauce and palm sugar and stir into the curry with the spinach. Remove from the heat and stir in the bean sprouts.

5 Spoon the rice into serving bowls, ladle in the curry and top with bean sprouts and coriander if desired. Serve.

Do not shake the can of coconut milk; see step 3.

Smooth the top of the leftover curry paste with a clean spoon then drizzle with oil to cover. This will prevent mould growth.

To get maximum juice from your limes, microwave them, uncut, for 45–60 seconds on High/100% until warm. Halve and juice while warm.

Blackened fish with white bean puree

serves 4

2-3 limes, juiced
1 teaspoon smoked paprika
2 teaspoons ground coriander
2 tablespoons olive oil
4 x 200g snapper fillets, skin removed
2 tomatoes, quartered, seeds removed, diced
2 tablespoons basil leaves, shredded
extra virgin olive oil and crusty bread, to serve

White bean puree
400g can cannellini beans, rinsed and drained
1/4 cup ground almonds
1 tablespoon lemon juice
1 garlic clove, crushed
1/4 cup olive oil

1 Combine 1/3 cup lime juice, paprika, coriander, oil and salt and pepper in a ceramic dish. Add fish and turn to coat. Stand 10 minutes.

2 For the white bean puree, place all ingredients in a food processor and process to combine. Transfer to a bowl, season with salt and pepper, cover with plastic wrap and set aside.

3 Preheat a barbecue plate or large non-stick frying pan over high heat. Remove the fish from the marinade, cook 4 minutes each side or until cooked through.

4 Spoon the white bean puree onto serving plates, top with fish. Combine the tomato and basil and spoon over the fish. Drizzle with extra virgin olive oil. Serve with crusty bread if desired.

Blackened fish with white bean puree

My quick pumpkin soup

serves 4

1 tablespoon olive oil
2 brown onions, finely chopped
1 garlic clove, crushed
1 teaspoon caster sugar
1.5kg butternut pumpkin,
   peeled, chopped
2-3 cups chicken stock
1/2 teaspoon ground nutmeg
140ml can coconut cream (Ayam brand)
crostini, to serve

1 Combine oil, onion, garlic and
sugar in a large microwave-safe bowl.
Microwave, uncovered for 3 minutes on
High/100% or until soft. Add pumpkin,
cover with damp paper towel and
microwave for 8 minutes on High/100% or
until pumpkin is tender.

2 Meanwhile, bring 2 cups stock to
the boil in a saucepan over medium-high
heat. Add the pumpkin mixture, cook
for 5 minutes until stock returns
to the boil.

3 Blend or process the soup until
smooth. Stir in nutmeg and season with
salt and pepper. Return to the saucepan,
add coconut cream and extra stock if
necessary, stir until hot (do not boil).
Ladle into bowls and serve with
crostini.

*Freshly ground nutmeg really
lifts this recipe. Whole nutmeg is
available from spice shops and
gourmet food shops.*

Mushrooms with soft polenta

serves 4

12 small flat mushrooms
1/4 cup olive oil
1/4 cup honey
2 tablespoons balsamic vinegar

Soft polenta
2 cups water
1 cup milk
60g butter, chopped
1 cup instant polenta (cornmeal)
1/4 cup finely chopped pitted
   black olives
2 tablespoons chilli jam (see page 233)

1 Preheat oven to 230°C no fan/230°C
fan-forced. Place mushrooms in a large
baking dish. Combine oil, honey and
vinegar in a screw-top jar. Microwave
dressing without lid for 30 seconds on
High/100%. Season with salt and pepper
and shake again. Pour the dressing over
the mushrooms and turn to coat. Set
aside for 10 minutes.

2 Transfer mushrooms to the oven and
roast for 10 minutes or until tender.

3 For the soft polenta, combine water,
milk and butter in a medium saucepan.
Bring to the boil over high heat.
Add polenta in a thin, steady stream,
stirring constantly. Reduce heat to
low and cook, stirring constantly, for
5 minutes or until thickened. Stir in
the olives and chilli jam.

4 Spoon the polenta onto serving plates,
top with mushrooms and spoon over any
juices. Serve.

Pad Thai

serves 4

250g dried pad Thai rice stick noodles
1/4 cup fish sauce
2 tablespoons grated palm sugar or brown sugar
1 lemon, juiced
150g firm tofu, diced
2 tablespoons cornflour
2 tablespoons peanut oil
2 chicken breast fillets, thinly sliced across the grain
3 eschallots, peeled, thinly sliced
2 garlic cloves, crushed
1 small red chilli, finely chopped
1 small green chilli, finely chopped
2 eggs, lightly beaten
1/2 cup roasted peanuts, chopped
125g bean sprouts, trimmed
fried shallots (optional), coriander leaves and
    lemon wedges, to serve

1 Place noodles in a large bowl, cover with warm water and set aside for 5 minutes or until noodles are tender. Drain well. Combine fish sauce, palm sugar and 1/4 cup lemon juice in a jug, stir to dissolve the sugar. Set aside.

2 Place tofu and cornflour into a snap lock bag and shake gently to coat the tofu. Heat wok over medium-high heat until hot. Add 2 teaspoons oil and the tofu, stir-fry gently until the tofu is golden. Remove to a plate, then wipe the wok clean.

3 Heat the wok over high heat until hot. Add 1 tablespoon oil and swirl to coat the surface. Add the chicken, stir-fry until golden. Transfer to a plate. Add remaining 2 teaspoons oil, eschallots, garlic and chillies and stir-fry for 1 minute. Push to one side of the wok. Add the eggs and cook until slightly set. Use a wooden spoon to stir the egg until scrambled. Add the noodles (don't worry if they are stuck together), fish sauce mixture, peanuts, bean sprouts, chicken and tofu. Stir-fry 1-2 minutes or until heated through. Sprinkle with fried shallots and coriander and serve with lemon wedges.

To keep bean sprouts crisp, place them into a bowl of cold water when you return from shopping, cover and keep in the fridge for up to 5 days.

On a 4-hour stop-over in Thailand I decided to take myself off to a cooking class instead of filling in time at the airport. The panic of trying to get back into an airport I should never have left was worth it — I learnt the art of cooking pad Thai.

Minute steak with pepperonata

Minute steak with pepperonata

serves 4

1 tablespoon olive oil
8 small minute steaks
shoestring chips (see page 229), to serve

Pepperonata
1/4 cup extra virgin olive oil
1 small brown onion, finely chopped
2 garlic cloves, crushed
2 red capsicums, cut into strips
1 yellow capsicum, cut into strips
1 orange capsicum, cut into strips
400g can whole peeled tomatoes, chopped
1 teaspoon caster sugar
3 teaspoons red wine vinegar

1 For the pepperonata, heat half the oil in a non-stick frying pan over medium-low heat. Add onion and garlic, cook stirring 5 minutes or until onion softens. Stir in capsicums, cover and cook for 20 minutes or until tender. Add tomatoes, sugar and season with salt and pepper. Increase heat to medium-high, then cook, uncovered, stirring often for 8 minutes or until sauce has thickened. Add vinegar and cook 1 minute.

2 Heat oil in a frying pan over medium high heat, cook steaks, two at a time, for 30 seconds each side for medium or until cooked to your liking. Place onto serving plates, top with a spoonful of pepperonata and serve with shoestring chips.

If yellow and orange capsicums are not available use 2 more red ones.

 Pepperonata is one of my favourite things to make up in a big batch and keep stored in the fridge. It's delicious on a ham sandwich, over pasta or pan-fried haloumi, on a sausage bun...and the list goes on. It will keep for 2 to 3 weeks in an airtight container.

Finger-licking chicken drumsticks

serves 4

If drumsticks
are large, use a
sharp knife to
cut 2—3 slashes
almost down to
the bone at the
thickest part of
the drumstick.
This allows the
heat to penetrate
so it will cook
right through.

10-12 chicken drumsticks, skin on
1 tablespoon salt flakes
1 tablespoon garlic salt
1 tablespoon lemon pepper
1/2 teaspoon smoked paprika
1 large lemon, rind finely grated
2 tablespoons olive oil
1/2 cup self-raising flour
olive oil cooking spray

1 Preheat oven to 210°C no fan/210°C fan-forced. Grease a large roasting pan.

2 Place salt flakes, garlic salt, lemon pepper, paprika, lemon rind and oil in a jug. Stir to combine. Place chicken drumsticks in a single layer on a large tray. Pour the oil mixture over the chicken. Rub into chicken to coat.

3 Place the flour in a large snap lock bag. Add drumsticks, one at a time, and toss to coat. Arrange drumsticks in roasting pan. Spray both sides lightly with oil. Roast for 30-35 minutes or until golden and cooked through. Serve with broccoli or beans with garlic hazelnut crumbs (see page 245).

Whenever I make
these there are
never any
leftovers, and
everyone wants
the recipe. Perfect
for dinner, picnics
or when you have
to take a plate.

Finger-licking chicken drumsticks

Red curry broth

Red curry broth

Serves 4

1 tablespoon peanut oil
400g chicken breast fillet, thinly sliced across the grain
1/4 cup red curry paste
5 green onions, thinly sliced
400ml can coconut milk
2 cups chicken stock
1 cup water
200g fresh thin rice noodles
1 bunch gai lum, trimmed, stalks diagonally sliced,
   leaves shredded
coriander leaves and lime wedges, to serve

1 Heat a wok over high heat until hot. Add 2 teaspoons oil and
swirl to coat the wok. Add half the chicken and stir-fry for
1 minute until light golden. Transfer to a plate. Repeat with
oil and remaining chicken.

2 Add curry paste and green onions to the wok, stir over medium
heat for 1-2 minutes or until aromatic. Add coconut milk, stock
and water. Bring to a simmer.

3 Add noodles, gai lum stalks and chicken to wok. Cook for 2-3 minutes
or until gai lum is tender.

4 Add gai lum leaves and stir until leaves wilt. Ladle into bowls.
Top with coriander. Serve with lime wedges.

Fresh rice noodles are not always available. You can use dried pad Thai noodles instead, but pre-soak them first.

Gai lum is also known as Chinese broccoli. It's part of the
Asian greens family. The leaves and stems are slightly thicker
than choy sum and the flowers are white. To store, wrap in
damp paper towels and place in a freezer bag in the crisper
section of the fridge. Always trim and discard 1—2 cm off
the stems. I like to separate the stems and leaves as the stems
require longer cooking.

As I have a Hungarian background, this was a regular mid-week meal growing up. I still ask Mum to make it when I go home for dinner. These potatoes are amazing. If left a little long in the pan they become really crispy.

Veal scallopine with potatoes and fennel salad

serves 4

1/4 cup plain flour
1/4 cup self-raising flour
1 1/2 cups fresh white breadcrumbs
2 eggs
4 x 140g veal steaks
olive oil, for cooking
4 sebago potatoes, peeled, cut into 3cm pieces

Fennel salad
2 small bulbs fennel
1 pink lady apple
1 small red onion
1 cup flat-leaf parsley leaves, roughly chopped
50g parmesan cheese, shaved
2 tablespoons extra virgin olive oil
2 tablespoons apple juice

It's important to keep the veal in a single layer as stacking the veal will compact the breadcrumbs, making them moist and they won't crisp up as well when frying.

1 Combine the flours on one plate and place the breadcrumbs on another. Lightly beat eggs in a shallow dish. Dip the veal steaks, one at a time, into the flour, shaking off the excess. Coat in the egg, allowing excess to drain off, then coat both sides with breadcrumbs, using fingertips to press the crumbs on.

2 Place the veal on a tray in a single layer. Cover and refrigerate 30 minutes (this helps hold breadcrumbs in place when cooking).

3 Meanwhile, cook the potatoes in a saucepan of boiling salted water until just tender. Preheat oven to 160°C no fan/150°C fan-forced.

4 For the fennel salad, thinly slice the fennel, apple and red onion (a mandolin is the easiest way) and place in a bowl with the parsley and parmesan. Combine olive oil and apple juice and drizzle over the salad just before serving. Season and toss gently to combine.

5 Cover the base of a large non-stick frying pan with oil and heat over medium heat. Cook the veal, in batches, for 2-3 minutes each side or until golden. Place on a wire rack and keep warm in the oven.

6 Drain the potatoes and add to the hot frying pan (with oil and crisp breadcrumbs left in the base). Cook over high heat until well coated in the crumbs. Serve with veal scallopine and shaved fennel salad.

Veal scallopine with potatoes and fennel salad

Macaroni Milano

Macaroni Milano

serves 4

From the butcher or farmers market — the better the sausages, the better the flavour of this dish.

500g good-quality Italian sausages
2 tablespoons olive oil
1 brown onion, halved, thinly sliced
1 large garlic clove, crushed
1/4 teaspoon dried chilli flakes
1 cup tomato passata sauce (see page 222)
1 cup beef stock
400g macaroni or rigatoni pasta
1/4 cup thickened cream
1/4 cup mascarpone
1/2 cup flat-leaf parsley leaves, chopped
50g parmesan cheese, grated
grated parmesan cheese, to serve

1 Use a sharp knife to split the sausage casings, then remove and discard the casings. Roughly chop the sausage meat.

2 Heat oil in a large frying pan over medium heat. Add onions and cook, stirring occasionally, for 4-5 minutes or until light golden. Increase the heat to high, add sausage meat to pan and cook for 3-4 minutes, breaking the meat up with a wooden spoon, until browned. Add garlic and chilli and cook, stirring, for 1 minute.

3 Stir in the passata and stock. Reduce the heat to medium-low and cook for 10-15 minutes or until sauce has thickened slightly.

4 Meanwhile, cook pasta in a large saucepan of boiling salted water until al dente. Drain and return to the hot saucepan.

5 Combine the cream, mascarpone and parsley and stir into the meat sauce. Add the meat sauce and parmesan to the pasta, toss over low heat until well combined. Season with salt and pepper. Serve.

Chorizo, spinach and lemon risotto

serves 4

4 chorizo sausages
1 tablespoon olive oil
1 red onion, halved, thinly sliced
2 cups arborio rice
4 cups chicken stock
1 bunch English spinach, shredded
2 tablespoons flat-leaf parsley leaves, chopped
1 lemon, rind finely grated
50g parmesan cheese, finely grated

1 Preheat oven to 180°C no fan/160°C fan-forced. Use a sharp knife to split sausage casings, remove and discard the casings. Roughly chop the sausage meat.

2 Heat the oil in an ovenproof saucepan over medium heat. Add the sausage meat and onion and cook, stirring occasionally, for 4-5 minutes until light golden. Add the rice and stir to coat. Add the stock and bring to the boil.

3 Remove the pan from the heat, cover with tight-fitting lid or foil. Transfer to the oven and bake for 18-20 minutes or until the stock is almost absorbed. Remove from the oven.

4 Stir in the spinach and parsley. Cover and stand for 1-2 minutes until spinach has wilted. Stir in the lemon rind and parmesan, then season with salt and pepper. Serve.

 If you don't have a saucepan that can be used on both the stove top and in the oven, cook steps 1 and 2 in a saucepan, then transfer the mixture to an ovenproof casserole dish to complete steps 3 and 4.

Chorizo, spinach and lemon risotto

Pan-seared fish with lentil and watercress salad

Pan-seared fish with lentil and watercress salad

serves 4

2 tablespoons extra virgin olive oil
1 red chilli, chopped
1 garlic clove, crushed
4 x 150g yellowtail kingfish fillets, skin on
  (or any firm white fish such as snapper, silver trevally, warehou)
80g soft goats cheese

Lentil and watercress salad
2 tablespoons extra virgin olive oil
3 teaspoons red wine vinegar
1 teaspoon Dijon mustard
1/2 small red onion, finely chopped
400g can brown lentils, rinsed and well drained
100g roasted capsicum, cut into strips (see page 234)
1 small bunch watercress, sprigs picked

1 For the lentil and watercress salad, whisk oil, vinegar, mustard and salt and pepper in a large bowl until well combined. Add onion and lentils and stir to coat. Cover and set aside for 10 minutes. Add capsicum and watercress just before serving and toss to combine.

2 Meanwhile, heat oil, chilli and garlic in a non-stick frying pan over medium-high heat. Season the fish with salt and pepper and pan-fry 3-4 minutes each side or until cooked through.

3 Divide the salad among serving plates, dollop with goats cheese and top with fish. Serve.

 Soft goats cheese is available from delis and large supermarkets in tubs. Marinated goats cheese or feta are suitable substitutes.

Potato and sweet onion frittata

serves 4

2 brown onions, halved, thinly sliced
800g unpeeled desiree potatoes, cut into 2cm pieces
2 tablespoons olive oil
1 cup frozen peas
125g mozzarella cheese, grated
7 fresh free-range eggs, at room temperature
1/4 cup flat-leaf parsley leaves, roughly chopped
100g fresh ricotta cheese

1 Place onions in a microwave-safe bowl, cover with paper towel and microwave on High/100% for 2-3 minutes or until soft. Rinse potatoes and place in a shallow microwave-safe dish no more than two layers deep. Cover and microwave on High/100% for 4-6 minutes or until almost tender. Drain and set aside.

2 Heat half the oil in a heavy-based 5cm-deep, 20cm (base) non-stick frying pan over medium heat. Add warm onions, cook stirring for 5 minutes until light golden. Remove onions to a plate. Add remaining oil and hot potatoes to the hot pan, cook, shaking the pan, for 8 minutes until potatoes are light golden. Return the onion to the pan, add peas and spread over the base of the pan. Sprinkle with the mozzarella. Reduce heat to medium-low.

3 Whisk the eggs in a bowl until well combined. Add parsley and season with pepper (no salt as this will cause the egg to weep). Pour the egg mixture over the potato mixture, gently shake the pan to allow the egg to run between the potato. Cook for 10 minutes or until the base and edges are firm but the top still a little soft. Remove from the heat. Spoon large dollops of ricotta over top of the frittata.

4 Preheat a grill on medium. Place the frittata (still in the frying pan) under the grill and cook for 5 minutes or until top is firm and light golden. Season with salt and pepper. Loosen the edge, cut into wedges and serve.

Potato and sweet onion frittata

Prosciutto-wrapped sausages with squashed potatoes

Prosciutto-wrapped sausages with squashed potatoes

serves 4

16 pork chipolata sausages
8 thin slices prosciutto or bacon, halved lengthways
2 tablespoons wholegrain mustard
1 garlic clove, crushed
2 tablespoons maple syrup
1 tablespoon olive oil
squashed potatoes (see page 227), to serve
steamed vegetables or cucumber and radish salad (see page 20),
   to serve

1 Preheat oven to 200°C no fan/200°C fan-forced.

2 Wrap 1 piece of prosciutto around each sausage and secure with
a toothpick if required. Combine mustard, garlic and maple syrup
in a shallow ceramic dish. Add sausages and turn to coat.

3 Heat oil in an ovenproof frying pan over medium-high heat. Add
sausages and cook for 3-4 minutes, turning often until light golden.
Remove pan from heat, pour the mustard marinade over the sausages
then transfer the pan to the oven. Roast a further 8-10 minutes or
until sausages are cooked through. Serve with squashed potatoes and
steamed vegetables or cucumber and radish salad if desired.

These are not just for the kids. Sausages are up there with lamb on my list of favourites. You can't go past those from the local butcher or farmers market!

If your frying pans are not ovenproof, transfer sausages to a roasting pan, pour the marinade over, then roast.

Coconut prawns with wok-tossed beans

serves 4

1 cup rice flour
2 eggs, lightly beaten
2 cups shredded coconut
24 (about 1kg) green king prawns,
  peeled with tails intact, deveined
vegetable or peanut oil, to deep-fry
lime wedges, to serve

Wok-tossed beans
2 garlic cloves, peeled
2 small red chillies, roughly chopped
1cm piece fresh ginger, peeled, roughly chopped
1 teaspoon white sugar
1 teaspoon sea salt flakes
1/2 cup desiccated or shredded coconut
2 teaspoons peanut oil
1 bunch snake beans, trimmed, cut into 6cm lengths

These wok-tossed beans are delicious served with almost any dish.

1 Place the rice flour, egg and coconut in separate bowls. Coat one prawn at a time in the flour, shaking off any excess. Dip into the egg, then press firmly into the coconut to evenly coat. Insert pre-soaked short bamboo skewers along the back of each prawn. Preheat oven to 160°C no fan/150°C fan-forced.

You can coat the prawns with the flour, egg and coconut up to 2 hours ahead.

2 Half fill a saucepan or wok with oil and heat over medium heat until hot. Cook prawns, in batches, for 2 minutes or until golden. Transfer to a wire rack over baking tray. Keep warm on rack in the oven.

3 For the wok-tossed beans, using a mortar and pestle or small food processor, pound or process the garlic, chilli, ginger, sugar, salt and coconut until it forms a paste.

4 Heat a wok over high heat until hot. Add the peanut oil and swirl to coat the wok. Add snake beans and stir-fry for 1-2 minutes until they start to change colour. Add the coconut mixture and stir-fry 1-2 minutes or until beans are tender. Serve with coconut prawns and lime wedges.

Coconut prawns with wok-tossed beans

Poached eggs with Worcestershire mushrooms

Poached eggs with Worcestershire mushrooms

serves 2

1 tablespoon white vinegar
4 fresh free-range eggs
    at room temperature
hot buttered toast, to serve

Worcestershire mushrooms
30g butter
400g mixed mushrooms (like swiss
    browns, shiitake, button), sliced
3 teaspoons Worcestershire sauce

1 Almost fill a 5cm-deep frying pan or saucepan with water (do not add salt as this will toughen the egg). Add vinegar and bring to simmer (small bubbles should break the water surface).

2 Stir the water to create a gentle whirlpool (this prevents eggs dropping to the base of the pan and sticking). Crack the egg into a small ramekin or bowl (to ensure it's fresh).

3 With the lip of the bowl right on the surface where the water is bubbling, slowly tip the egg into the water and stir gently to continue the whirlpool effect. Make sure the egg is completely covered with water and the water is moving. Repeat with remaining eggs, cooking no more than four at once.

4 Cook eggs for 1 1/2-2 minutes, then use a slotted spoon to remove the egg. Gently press the yolk to check if it's cooked to your liking. Place the spoon onto paper towel to allow any water to drain.

5 For the Worcestershire mushrooms, melt butter in a frying pan over high heat, add the mushrooms and saute 3-4 minutes or until tender. Add the Worcestershire sauce, season with salt and pepper and stir to combine.

6 Spoon the mushrooms onto the toast, top with eggs, season with salt and pepper and serve.

Microwave poached eggs

1 Lightly grease a microwave-safe ramekin or teacup. Crack the egg into the ramekin or cup.

2 Pierce the yolk carefully with a toothpick (this prevents yolk membrane from popping). Do not add salt.

3 Cover with a piece of damp paper towel, elevate on a microwave-safe rack or upturned plate so it sits 2cm off the turntable.

4 Cook 1 egg on Medium-low/Defrost/30% for 45-60 seconds (eggs should be slightly undercooked to your liking as they will continue to cook on standing). Allow to stand for 30 seconds. Season with salt and pepper and serve on hot buttered toast.

Cook 2 eggs for 1 1/2-2 minutes on Medium-low/Defrost/30%
Cook 4 eggs for 3-4 minutes on Medium-low/Defrost/30%

 Both these methods produce great results. The secret is really fresh eggs!

Not far from
where I live is the
most amazing
little Indonesian
restaurant and I
frequently visit it.
Slammet makes
the best satay I
have ever eaten
but this is a very
very close second.

Peanut sauce will
keep for 4 weeks
in an airtight
container in
the fridge.

Indonesian satay with peanut sauce

serves 6

4 large garlic cloves, crushed
1 small brown onion, grated
1/2 cup kecap manis (ABC brand)
2 tablespoons peanut oil
2 teaspoons caster sugar
1/2 teaspoon salt
1kg chicken thigh fillet or rump steak,
    cut into bite-sized pieces
steamed jasmine rice and wok-tossed beans (see page 58),
    to serve (optional)

Peanut sauce
1 tablespoons peanut oil
1 brown onion, finely chopped
3 small red chillies, finely chopped
4 large garlic cloves, crushed
2 teaspoons ground coriander
375g jar crunchy peanut butter (Kraft brand)
1 1/2 cups coconut milk
2 tablespoons kecap manis
1 tablespoon grated palm sugar
1 lime, juiced

1 Combine the garlic, onion, kecap manis, oil, sugar and salt in a
large snap lock bag, add the chicken or beef and rub well to coat.
Refrigerate 3 hours or overnight if time permits.

2 For the peanut sauce, heat the oil in a saucepan over medium heat.
Add the onion, chilli, garlic and coriander and cook for 2-3 minutes
until the onion is soft. Add the peanut butter and coconut milk,
then cook for 3-4 minutes until warm. Stir in the kecap manis,
palm sugar and 1 tablespoon lime juice. Taste and adjust seasoning
adding salt and sugar as desired.

3 Preheat a barbecue plate or grill to medium-high. Thread the
marinated chicken or beef onto skewers. Barbecue 5-8 minutes, turning
often until cooked through. Serve skewers with peanut sauce, steamed
rice and wok-tossed beans if desired.

Indonesian satay with peanut sauce

Fast inspirations

Moroccan-spiced chicken

Cut a chicken breast fillet in half to form two thin fillets, sprinkle with Moroccan spice and drizzle with olive oil. Pan-fry fillets until light golden. Add the juice of an orange, a little chicken stock and a handful of dried currants. Simmer until cooked through. Serve with couscous (see page 225).

Mustard veal

Spread both sides of veal steaks with Dijon mustard, coat in plain flour and pan-fry in olive oil until light golden. Add a little chicken stock to the pan and simmer for a few minutes, turning the veal occasionally, until sauce thickens slightly. Serve with mashed potato (see page 226).

Asian vegetable omelette

Cook an omelette (see page 121). Stir-fry julienne carrots, red capsicum and snow peas until tender but crisp. Add a handful of bean sprouts and a drizzle of kecap manis. Spoon onto the omelette and fold over to serve.

10-minute sausage pasta

Roughly chop Italian sausages and sauté with brown onion and garlic in olive oil until light golden. Add a can diced tomatoes, chopped basil and simmer until sauce has thickened. Serve over pasta.

Sweet and sour pork skewers

Cut a pork fillet into strips and thread onto skewers with wedges of fresh pineapple and chopped red capsicum. Brush with purchased sweet and sour sauce and barbecue or grill until cooked. Serve with jasmine rice.

Vegetarian pizza

Spread pre-bought pizza base with hummus dip, top with shredded English spinach and chopped semi-dried tomatoes. Crack 2-3 eggs over the pizza and crumble over fresh ricotta cheese. Bake in a hot oven until base is crisp and eggs are cooked to your liking.

Chicken and tomato pasta bake

Toss the shredded meat from a barbecue or roast chicken with cooked macaroni and tomato passata sauce (see page 222). Spoon into a baking dish, top with chopped olives and parsley. Sprinkle over grated cheese and bake until piping hot.

Easy salmon pie

Place a fillet of salmon onto a piece of purchased puffed pastry. Top with basil leaves, finely grated lemon rind and chopped green onions. Season with salt and pepper, then wrap tightly in the pastry. Score the pastry top and brush with beaten egg. Bake in hot oven for 10-15 minutes until golden and puffed. Serve with steamed vegetables.

San choy bau

Saute pork mince in peanut oil with chopped green onions, garlic, ginger and kecap manis. Spoon into crisp iceberg lettuce cups. Top with bean sprouts and chopped peanuts.

Chicken, avocado and beetroot panini

Flatten a chicken thigh fillet. Pan-fry or barbecue the chicken
with sliced red onion and bacon. Place between a toasted
torpedo roll along with sliced avocado, watercress sprigs and
purchased beetroot dip or chutney.

Vietnamese sesame chicken stir-fry

Shred pan-fried chicken and stir-fry with lots of shredded
snow peas and green onions. Toss with cooked fresh egg noodles,
sprinkle with toasted sesame seeds. Drizzle with nuoc cham
(see page 242).

Honey mustard crumbed lamb

Combine Dijon mustard, honey and finely chopped garlic, and
spread over both sides of lamb cutlets. Coat the cutlets
in fresh breadcrumbs and pan-fry until golden and tender.
Serve with lemon-scented broccoli (see page 244).

Fresh

Fresh. Possibly the most overused word in the food and cooking lexicon. I am a big believer that cooking from scratch with as many fresh ingredients as possible is a good thing. The fewer processed foods we consume the better off we will be. We are all so obsessed with fat and carbohydrate that we often forget to look out for preservatives and additives. The following recipes will inspire you to increase the number of fresh ingredients you use every day, but they still keep the focus on getting a great meal on the table without too much fuss.

Rice paper rolls with hoisin dipping sauce

makes 12

100g dried rice vermicelli noodles
500g cooked prawns, peeled, deveined
2 cups shredded cooked chicken
1 cup fresh mint leaves
100g bean sprouts, trimmed
1 large carrot, peeled, grated
1 bunch garlic chives
375g packet round rice paper wrappers

Hoisin dipping sauce
3/4 cup hoisin sauce (Lee Kum Kee brand)
1/3 cup smooth peanut butter (Kraft brand)
2 tablespoons boiling water
1/3 cup roasted salted peanuts, chopped

1 For the hoisin dipping sauce, combine all ingredients in a saucepan over medium heat. Cook, stirring, for 5 minutes or until hot, adding more water if needed (the sauce should be the consistency of thickened cream). Set aside to cool.

2 Soak the noodles, following packet directions. Drain. Refresh in cold water.

3 Split the prawns in half lengthways with a sharp knife. Arrange prawns, noodles, chicken, mint, sprouts, carrot and chives in separate piles on platter.

4 Half fill a shallow dish with lukewarm water. Dip one wrapper into water, then place on bench and stand for 30 seconds or until soft enough to roll without splitting.

5 Place two prawn halves along one edge of the wrapper. Top with a little chicken, noodles, mint, sprouts, carrot and chives (don't overfill or the rolls will split). Roll up, folding edges in. Cover with a cloth. Repeat with remaining ingredients.

6 Serve rice paper rolls fresh, or deep-fried until golden, with hoisin dipping sauce and nuoc cham (see page 242).

Rice paper rolls with hoisin dipping sauce

Crispy-skin duck with pink grapefruit and avocado salad

Crispy-skin duck with pink grapefruit and avocado salad

serves 4

4 fresh duck marylands
olive oil
chilli jam (see page 233), to serve

Pink grapefruit and avocado salad
2 pink grapefruit
2 tablespoons extra virgin olive oil
1 teaspoon Dijon mustard
1/4 teaspoon caster sugar
100g baby spinach leaves
1 large ripe avocado, halved, stone removed,
  peeled, thinly sliced

1 Preheat oven to 200°C no fan/180°C fan-forced.

2 For the pink grapefruit and avocado salad, use a small sharp knife to remove the skin and white pith from the grapefruit. Holding the grapefruit over a large bowl to catch juices, segment the fruit. Place the grapefruit segments on a plate and squeeze the membrane over the bowl to release any remaining juices. Add the oil, mustard, sugar and salt and pepper to the bowl and whisk to combine. Just before serving, add the grapefruit segments, spinach and avocado and toss gently to coat.

3 Use a sharp knife to score the duck skin. Rub lightly with olive oil and season with salt and pepper. Heat a large ovenproof frying pan over high heat. Cook the duck skin-side down for 2-3 minutes until golden, turn and cook for 2 minutes. Transfer to the oven and roast for 8 minutes for medium or until cooked to your liking. Cover and set aside to rest for 5-10 minutes.

4 Pile the salad onto serving plates, top with duck and serve with a dollop of chilli jam.

Pink grapefruit are at their best from August through to the end of November. They are sweeter than the yellow variety, and a good source of the powerful antioxidant lycopene.

Peppered beef with gourmet mushrooms

serves 4

60g butter, melted
3 teaspoons Dijon mustard
500g mixed mushrooms (like button, swiss brown, shiitake
  and oyster), thickly sliced
4 eschallots, peeled, thinly sliced
1 tablespoon pink peppercorns
1 tablespoon black peppercorns
2 tablespoons fresh thyme leaves
1 tablespoon olive oil
1kg eye fillet beef, trimmed
basil pesto beans (see page 244), to serve

1 Preheat oven to 200°C no fan/190°C fan-forced. Combine butter and mustard in a bowl, add mushrooms and eschallots and stir to coat. Spoon mushrooms and eschallots over the base of a large roasting pan, season with salt and pepper.

2 Pound the peppercorns in a mortar with the pestle until coarsely ground. Add thyme leaves and sprinkle mixture onto a piece of baking paper. Brush beef with oil then roll in pepper mixture. Tie the beef at 3cm intervals with unwaxed string.

3 Heat a non-stick frying pan over high heat. Add the beef fillet and cook, turning occasionally, for 5 minutes or until it is browned all over. Place beef on a rack over the mushrooms. Roast for 25-30 minutes for medium or until cooked to your liking.

4 Loosely cover beef and allow to stand for 15 minutes to rest. Slice the beef and spoon over the mushrooms and pan juices. Serve with basil pesto beans.

Trim the silvery sinew from the beef. If left on it will cause the beef to shrink during cooking.

Eschallots, also known as shallots, are very small brown onions with a thin papery reddish-brown skin. They have a mild onion flavour and are very popular in both Asian and French cuisine. You will find them in greengrocers and supermarkets, and although a little fiddly to peel they are worth the effort. Red onion is a suitable alternative.

Peppered beef with gourmet mushrooms

Salad niçoise

Salad niçoise

serves 4

400g small kipfler or pink fir potatoes, scrubbed
200g small green beans, trimmed
2 tablespoons olive oil
400g pieces fresh tuna, bloodline removed,
  cut into cubes
4 ripe tomatoes, cut into wedges
12 niçoise olives
1 tablespoon capers
4 medium boiled eggs (see page 221)
French bread, to serve

Dressing
100ml extra virgin olive oil
1/2 lemon, juiced
2 anchovy fillets, finely chopped
2 teaspoons Dijon mustard

1 Cook the potatoes in a saucepan of boiling, salted water for 8-10 minutes until tender, adding the beans to the boiling salted water for the last minute. Drain. Set the potatoes aside to cool, then slice. Meanwhile, refresh the beans immediately in cold water, pat dry with paper towels.

2 Heat the oil in a frying pan over medium-high heat. Season the tuna with salt and pepper and add to the pan, cook for 1-2 minutes, tossing often, until seared.

3 For the dressing, place all the ingredients with salt and pepper in a screw-top jar and shake well to combine.

4 Combine the potatoes, beans, tomatoes, olives, capers and tuna in a bowl. Pour the dressing over and toss gently to combine. Divide salad among serving bowls. Peel eggs then cut into quarters and arrange on the salad. Season with pepper and serve with French bread.

 Niçoise olives are a small purplish-black olive, traditionally used in salad niçoise. They are available in jars in brine from delis and specialty food stores. Kalamata olives are a suitable substitute.

This popular French classic not only tastes great but is a good way to increase the all-important fish in our diet. For an even faster version, use canned tuna instead of fresh.

Char-grilled vegetable pies

serves 4

olive oil cooking spray
400g piece butternut pumpkin, cut into 5mm slices
1 small eggplant, cut into 5mm slices
1 red capsicum, quartered, seeds removed
1 yellow capsicum, quartered, seeds removed
2 small zucchini, halved crossways,
   thinly sliced lengthways
200g haloumi, thinly sliced
1 sheet frozen ready-rolled shortcrust pastry,
   partially thawed
1/4 cup basil pesto (see page 236)
2 sheets frozen ready-rolled puff pastry,
   partially thawed

1 Preheat a barbecue grill or char-grill pan on high until hot. Spray both sides of vegetables and haloumi with oil spray. Char-grill the pumpkin for 3-4 minutes each side. Remove to a plate, cover with foil (this helps complete cooking of the pumpkin so it's tender right through to the centre).

2 Char-grill the eggplant, capsicum and zucchini for 5 minutes each side or until tender. Remove to a board. Peel any black skin from capsicum and cut into thick strips. Char-grill haloumi for 2-3 minutes each side until light golden.

3 Preheat oven and a flat baking tray to 230°C no fan/220°C fan-forced. Place a sheet of baking paper onto a large chopping board. Cut shortcrust pastry in half and place both pieces onto the baking paper. Spread pesto over the pastry leaving a 1cm border around each edge. Top with char-grilled vegetables and haloumi. Place one sheet puff pastry over each pie. Press pastry edges together to seal, trimming excess pastry.

4 Brush the top of the pies with cold water and sprinkle with salt and cracked black pepper. Score the top of each pie at 1cm intervals. Carefully slide the pies (still on the baking paper) onto the hot tray. Bake for 25-30 minutes or until puffed and golden. Cut in half and serve hot or cold.

Char-grilled vegetable pies

Balti lamb curry

Balti lamb curry

serves 4

3/4 cup balti curry paste ◀ ·······

1kg lamb neck fillet or shoulder, cut into 3cm cubes
2 tablespoons ghee
1 large brown onion, finely chopped
3 large garlic cloves, crushed
3 teaspoons garam masala
coriander leaves and warm chapatti, to serve

1 Preheat oven to 130°C no fan/120°C fan-forced. Combine 1/4 cup curry paste and 1 1/2 cups water in an ovenproof casserole dish. Whisk to dissolve the curry paste. Add the lamb and stir to combine. The lamb should be covered with the curry water.

2 Cover the dish with a tight-fitting lid or a double layer of foil and bake for 2 1/2-3 hours or until lamb is tender. Remove from the oven, strain the meat, reserving 1 1/3 cups of the cooking liquid. (You can prepare the curry to the end of this step up to 4 days ahead.)

3 Melt the ghee in a wok over medium heat. Add the onion, garlic and garam masala and cook, stirring occasionally, for 4 minutes or until onion is softened. Stir in the remaining 1/2 cup curry paste, cook, stirring, for 1 minute or until aromatic.

4 Increase the heat to medium-high, add the lamb and stir to coat in curry paste mixture. Reduce heat to low, add reserved cooking liquid. Simmer, uncovered, for 10 minutes or until warmed through. Top with coriander leaves and serve with warm chapatti.

Balti curry paste is a tomato-based paste, flavoured with coriander and chilli. It has a heat rating of mild to medium.

Balti curries are mild, and this ancient method of cooking delivers the most tender curry you will ever eat. I replace the lamb with pork scotch fillet when it's cheaper.

 Ghee is clarified butter, available near the butter in the supermarket. It won't burn over high heat, making it great for all sorts of things from curries to pancakes and pikelets.

Beetroot dip

serves 8

3 medium fresh beetroot
1 head garlic
olive oil cooking spray
1 tablespoon red wine vinegar
$1/4$ cup extra virgin olive oil
1 teaspoon horseradish cream

1 Preheat oven to 210°C no fan/200°C fan-forced. Trim beetroot, leaving 1cm of the stalk attached. Cut 5mm off the top of the head of garlic. Place beetroot and garlic onto a baking tray. Spray with oil. Roast for 30-40 minutes or until beetroot is tender. Set aside to cool.

2 Using a knife, peel the beetroot. Roughly chop the flesh and place into a food processor. Squeeze roasted soft flesh from the garlic head into the processor. Process until smooth.

3 Combine the vinegar, oil and horseradish in a jug. With the processor on, add vinegar mixture. Season dip with salt and pepper. Press a piece of plastic wrap onto the surface of the dip and refrigerate until ready to serve.

Orange hummus dip

serves 8

100ml extra virgin olive oil
2 x 300g cans chickpeas, rinsed, drained
$1/4$ cup pine nuts, toasted
3 large oranges, rind finely grated, juiced
2 tablespoons tahini
4 garlic cloves, crushed
$1/2$ teaspoon cayenne pepper

1 Process oil, chickpeas, pine nuts, orange rind, $1/2$ cup orange juice, tahini, garlic and $1/4$ teaspoon of the cayenne pepper in a food processor until smooth.

2 Taste and season with salt, adding the remaining cayenne pepper, if desired. Press a piece of plastic wrap onto the surface of the dip and refrigerate until ready to serve.

Roasted egglant dip

serves 8

2 medium (350g each) eggplant
6 garlic cloves, skin on
2 tablespoons tahini
2 tablespoons extra virgin olive oil
4 green onions, finely chopped
2 tablespoons Greek-style yoghurt
$1/2$ lemon, juiced

1 Preheat oven to 220°C no fan/200°C fan-forced. Pierce each eggplant six times with a fork, place into a roasting pan with the garlic. Roast for 30-40 minutes or until eggplant is soft. Set aside to cool.

2 Cut the eggplant in half lengthways. Using a metal spoon, scoop the flesh into a bowl. Stir in the tahini, oil, green onions, yoghurt and 2 tablespoons lemon juice.

3 Squeeze the roasted soft flesh from garlic and mash with a fork until smooth, stir into the dip. Season with salt and pepper. Press a piece of plastic wrap onto the surface of the dip and refrigerate until ready to serve.

Clockwise from back: Beetroot dip; Orange hummus dip; and Roasted eggplant dip

Lasagne

Lasagne

serves 6

1 quantity bechamel sauce (see page 243)
250g dried lasagne pasta sheets
1 quantity Bolognese sauce (see page 223), warm
8 balls bocconcini cheese, torn in half
100g mozzarella cheese, coarsely grated

1 Preheat oven to 190°C no fan/180°C fan-forced. Grease a 3-litre capacity, 7cm-deep, 18cm x 25cm (base) rectangular baking dish.

2 Spread $1/3$ cup warm bechamel sauce over the base of dish (this prevents dried pasta sticking to the base). Cover with one layer pasta sheets, breaking to fit if necessary. Top with one-third of the Bolognese sauce and one-third of the remaining bechamel sauce. Repeat layering twice with the pasta and sauces, finishing with bechamel sauce. Top with bocconcini and mozzarella.

3 Place the dish onto a baking tray, to catch any spills. Bake, uncovered, for 45-50 minutes or until golden and bubbling around the edges. Stand lasagne for 5 minutes before serving.

A good Bolognese sauce is the base to many great dishes. The lasagne here and the following three recipes, are just four of my all-time faves with Bolognese!

 The right size dish is essential for success. To find out the capacity, fill the dish with water, counting the number of cups (or litres). A 3-litre dish will take 12 cups/3 litres of water!

Free-form Bolognese pie

serves 4

1 sheet shortcrust pastry,
  partially thawed
3 cups Bolognese sauce (see page 223),
  at room temperature
1 sheet puff pastry, partially thawed
cos salad (see page 110) or parmesan carrots (see page 246),
  to serve

1 Preheat the oven and a flat baking tray to 200°C no fan/
180°C fan-forced.

2 Place the shortcrust pastry onto a sheet of baking paper.
Top with the bolognese sauce leaving a 2cm border around all
the edges. Place the puff pastry over the top and press edges
down to secure. Cut slits at 1cm intervals in the top of the pie.
Brush the top with water and sprinkle with salt and pepper.

3 Carefully lift the pie, still on the baking paper, onto the
hot tray. Bake for 25-30 minutes or until golden and puffed.
Serve with cos salad or parmesan carrots.

You can make this pie up to the end of this step and freeze it. Allow to partially thaw before cooking at 180°C no fan/ 160°C fan-forced for 45–50 minutes.

Pastitsio

serves 6

400g macaroni pasta
1 quantity Bolognese sauce
  (see page 223), warm
2 eggs, lightly beaten
1 cup finely grated tasty cheese
1 quantity bechamel sauce
  (see page 243), warm

1 Preheat oven to 200°C no fan/180°C
fan-forced. Grease a 3-litre capacity,
7cm-deep, 18cm x 25cm (base) rectangular
baking dish.

2 Cook the pasta in a saucepan of
boiling salted water until al dente.
Drain and return to the hot saucepan.
Add the Bolognese sauce and stir to
combine. Spoon the mixture into the
baking dish.

3 Stir eggs and cheese into the
bechamel sauce then spread over the
pasta mixture. (You can make the
pastitsio to the end of this step up
to 2 days ahead. Cover and refrigerate,
then bake when you're ready.)

4 Place the dish onto a baking tray,
to catch any spills. Bake, uncovered,
for 45-50 minutes or until golden and
bubbling around the edges. Serve.

Cottage pie

serves 6

2 carrots, peeled, grated
2 stalks celery, finely chopped
2 zucchini, grated
1 roasted red capsicum
  (see page 234), chopped
1 quantity Bolognese sauce
  (see page 223), at room temperature
1 quantity mashed potato
  (see page 226), warm
1 cup finely grated tasty cheese

1 Preheat oven to 200°C no fan/180°C
fan-forced. Grease a 2.5-litre capacity
baking dish.

2 Stir the carrot, celery, zucchini and
capsicum into Bolognese sauce. Spoon the
mixture into baking dish and dollop over
the mashed potato. Sprinkle with cheese.

3 Place the dish onto a baking tray, to
catch any spills. Bake, uncovered, for
45-50 minutes or until light golden and
bubbling around the edges. Serve.

Fresh pea and pancetta soup

serves 4

1.25kg fresh peas in the pod (4 cups shelled)
2 sprigs rosemary
2 sprigs flat-leaf parsley
4 cups chicken stock
2 tablespoons extra virgin olive oil
2 brown onions, finely chopped
2 large garlic cloves, crushed
2 stalks celery, finely chopped
100g thinly sliced hot pancetta, finely chopped
1/2 cup small pasta shapes
1 small lemon, rind finely grated, juiced
toasted crusty bread, to serve

1 Remove peas from pods. Place pea pods, rosemary and parsley sprigs in a saucepan. Add the stock, cover and bring to the boil over medium heat.

2 Meanwhile, heat oil in a large, heavy-based saucepan over medium heat. Add onions, garlic, celery and pancetta. Cook, stirring often, for 6 minutes or until onion is soft. Add peas and stir to coat. Strain the stock and pour it over the pea mixture. Simmer gently over medium heat for 10 minutes or until the peas are tender.

3 Cook the pasta in a saucepan of boiling salted water until al dente. Drain.

4 Ladle half the soup into a food processor or blender and process or blend until smooth. Stir pureed mixture back into the soup, then add lemon rind, 2 tablespoons lemon juice and the pasta. Season well with salt and pepper. Simmer over medium heat until heated through. Serve with toasted crusty bread.

Use the light green inner stalks of the celery. They are known as the heart and are much sweeter.

When I was growing up my Mum could never get me to eat my peas. I have to say, they are still not my favourite vegetable, but in this soup they are sensational. If you don't have time for shelling fresh peas, use 4 cups frozen ones.

Fresh pea and pancetta soup

Mediterranean vegetable pasta

Mediterranean vegetable pasta

serves 4

This is a great recipe to use up leftover vegetables and herbs.

1 red capsicum, cut into 3cm pieces
1 yellow capsicum, cut into 3cm pieces
2 carrots, peeled, halved, cut into 3cm pieces
1/4 small butternut pumpkin, cut into wedges
1 eggplant, cut into 3cm pieces
2 zucchini, halved, cut into 3cm pieces
1 red onion, cut into thin wedges
2 tablespoons olive oil
400g tagliatelle
2/3 cup kalamata olives
1 tablespoon capers, drained
1 cup fresh herbs (like basil, mint, thyme and flat-leaf parsley)
extra virgin olive oil and balsamic vinegar, to serve

1 Preheat oven to 230°C no fan/230°C fan-forced. Combine the capsicum, carrot, pumpkin, eggplant, zucchini and onion in a large, greased roasting pan. Drizzle with olive oil and season with salt and pepper, turning all the vegetables to coat. Roast for 20-30 minutes, turning the vegetables every 10 minutes until they are golden and tender.

2 Cook the pasta in a large saucepan of boiling salted water following packet directions until al dente. Drain and add to the hot roasting pan with the olives, capers and herbs, toss gently to combine. Season with salt and pepper.

3 Pile the pasta in serving bowls, drizzle with oil and balsamic vinegar and serve.

Poached salmon and Asian greens in soy broth

serves 4

Use the back of a heavy knife, charn (wok turner) or cleaver to bash the lemongrass until you can smell the sweet aroma.

2 cups chicken stock
2 cups water
3/4 cup shao hsing wine
2 tablespoons light soy sauce
1/4 cup kecap manis
2 tablespoons grated palm sugar
2 garlic cloves, sliced
5cm piece unpeeled ginger, sliced
1 stalk lemongrass, bruised
2 small red chillies, halved
1 star anise
2 cinnamon sticks, split lengthways
4 salmon fillets, skin removed
100g mushrooms (like shiitake or swiss brown), sliced
1 bunch gai lum, leaves and stems shredded

1 Combine the stock, water, shao hsing wine, soy, kecap manis, palm sugar, garlic, ginger, lemongrass, chilli, star anise and cinnamon sticks in a deep frying pan or wok over medium-high heat. Bring to the boil, reduce heat to medium-low and simmer for 20 minutes or until stock mixture has reduced slightly.

2 Reduce the heat to low, add the salmon and simmer gently for 5-10 minutes or until cooked to your liking.

3 Using a slotted spoon carefully remove the salmon to four shallow bowls; cover to keep warm.

4 Strain the stock mixture; return the stock to the pan and bring to the boil. Add the shiitake mushrooms and gai lum and simmer for 2-3 minutes until vegetables are just tender. Taste and adjust the seasoning (add palm sugar if it needs sweetening or soy for salt). Ladle the hot stock and vegetables over the salmon and serve.

This dish is glorious. It's light enough to enjoy all through summer and filling enough to satisfy through winter.

You can make the stock (step 1) days ahead, then simmer the salmon just before serving. You can replace the salmon with white fish or chicken breast.

Poached salmon with Asian greens in soy broth

Cranberry chilli lamb

serves 4

1/4 cup olive oil
1/3 cup cranberry jelly
1/4 cup chilli jam (see page 233)
2 large garlic cloves, crushed
2 tablespoons rosemary leaves
12 lamb cutlets
beans, asparagus and pine nut salad
   (see page 31), to serve

1 Combine oil, cranberry jelly, chilli
jam, garlic, rosemary and salt and
pepper in a jug. Whisk with a fork to
combine. Place the lamb in a ceramic
dish, pour over the marinade and turn
to coat. Cover and marinate 15 minutes.

2 Preheat a greased barbecue plate on
high, then reduce heat to medium-high.
Remove the lamb from the marinade,
reserving the marinade. Cook the lamb
on barbecue plate, basting with the
marinade, for 3-4 minutes on each
side for medium or until cooked to
your liking.

3 Serve the lamb with beans, asparagus
and pine nut salad.

Vietnamese beef pho

serves 4

500g beef eye fillet,
   very thinly sliced
1.5 litres beef stock
5 star anise
1 cinnamon stick, split lengthways
6cm piece fresh ginger, sliced
300g dried rice vermicelli noodles
2 tablespoons fish sauce
2 teaspoons grated palm sugar or
   brown sugar
2 tablespoons rice vinegar
6 green onions, thinly sliced
1/3 cup coriander leaves
100g bean sprouts, trimmed

1 Place the beef on a plate and freeze
for 1 hour or until partially frozen
(this makes it easier to thinly slice).
Thinly slice across the grain and set
aside to thaw.

2 Bring stock, star anise, cinnamon
stick and ginger to the boil in a
large saucepan. Reduce the heat to low.
Cover and cook for 30 minutes. Using a
slotted spoon, remove the star anise,
cinnamon stick and ginger.

3 Cook the noodles following packet
directions. Drain. Arrange the noodles
and raw beef in the base of warm
serving bowls.

4 Add the fish sauce, sugar and rice
vinegar to the stock mixture and bring
back to the boil. Ladle the boiling
stock mixture over the beef and noodles.
Combine the green onions, coriander and
bean sprouts, then pile on top of the
soup. Serve.

Herb chicken rissoles with avocado salsa

serves 4 as a main

2 tablespoons olive oil
3cm piece fresh ginger, peeled, grated
1 small red onion, grated
500g chicken breast mince
1 egg, lightly beaten
1 cup fresh breadcrumbs
1/4 cup fresh tarragon leaves, chopped
1/4 cup flat-leaf parsley leaves, chopped
1/4 cup chopped chives
2 tablespoons mango chutney
olive oil cooking spray

Avocado salsa
1 telegraph cucumber
1 large ripe firm avocado
1 tablespoon red wine vinegar
1 tablespoon extra virgin olive oil
pinch caster sugar

1 Heat oil in a large frying pan over medium-high heat. Add ginger and onion and cook, stirring occasionally, for 5 minutes or until onion is soft. Transfer to a bowl and allow to cool 10 minutes.

2 Add chicken mince, egg, breadcrumbs, tarragon, parsley, chives, mango chutney and salt and pepper to the onion mixture, and mix until well combined.

3 Shape mixture evenly into eight rissoles about 2cm thick. Place on a tray, cover and refrigerate for 30 minutes.

4 For the avocado salsa, cut the cucumber in half lengthways. Use a spoon to scoop out the seeds. Dice cucumber and avocado and place in a bowl. Combine the vinegar, oil, sugar, and salt and pepper in a jug, then pour over the avocado mixture. Toss gently to combine.

5 Heat a barbecue plate or non-stick frying pan on medium. Lightly spray both sides of the rissoles with oil and cook for 4 minutes each side or until golden and cooked through. Serve with avocado salsa.

These chicken rissoles are just as good served cold between pieces of toasted Turkish bread with whole egg mayonnaise, semi-dried tomatoes and baby spinach leaves.

Standing the rissoles for 30 minutes in the fridge allows the flavours to develop and helps them hold together during cooking.

Corn and zucchini fritter

Corn and zucchini fritter

serves 4 as main

500g (4 medium) zucchini, coarsely grated
400g (2 medium) sebago potatoes, peeled,
  coarsely grated
4 corn cobs, kernels removed
4 green onions, finely chopped
2 tablespoons flat-leaf parsley, chopped
1 cup besan (chickpea flour) or 1/2 cup plain flour
1 teaspoon baking powder
2 eggs, lightly whisked
2 tablespoons olive oil
baby rocket leaves and extra virgin olive oil, to serve

1 Squeeze the zucchini and potato with your hands to remove the
excess moisture. Transfer to a large bowl. Add corn, green onions
and parsley and stir to combine. Sift besan and baking powder together
over the vegetables, then stir to combine. Add egg, season with salt
and pepper, and mix well.

2 Heat the oil in a 25cm (base) non-stick frying pan over medium heat,
brushing the side of the pan with the warm oil. Spread the fritter
mixture evenly into the pan. Reduce heat to medium-low, cover and
cook for 15 minutes until base is golden and fritter is almost set.

3 Preheat the grill on medium. Remove cover from the frying pan,
then place pan under the grill. Cook for 8-10 minutes or until firm
in the centre and light golden.

4 Slide fritter onto a board, top with rocket, drizzle with olive oil,
season with salt and pepper and cut into wedges to serve.

Besan is available from health food stores. Keep the leftover flour in an airtight container in the freezer to prevent weevils.

Fritters are always popular and a great way to hide vegetables from the kids. This is a healthy version everyone will love.

Greek lamb with watermelon salad

serves 4

1/4 cup olive oil
1 large lemon, rind finely grated, juiced
2 garlic cloves, crushed
1 tablespoon dried oregano
1/2 teaspoon ground nutmeg
600g lamb backstrap or loin fillet

Watermelon salad
450g seedless watermelon, peeled, roughly chopped
100g Greek feta cheese, crumbled
1/3 cup walnuts, chopped
1/4 cup small mint leaves
2 tablespoons extra virgin olive oil
1 lime, juiced

1 Combine oil, lemon rind, 1/4 cup lemon juice, garlic, oregano, nutmeg
and salt and pepper in a jug. Whisk with a fork to combine. Arrange
lamb in a single layer in a ceramic dish, pour over the marinade and
turn to coat. Cover and refrigerate 30 minutes if time permits.

2 Preheat a greased barbecue plate on medium-high. Remove the lamb
from marinade. Cook the lamb for 4 minutes each side for medium or until
cooked to your liking. Cover and set aside to rest for 10 minutes.

3 For the watermelon salad, combine the watermelon, feta, walnuts and
mint in a bowl. Whisk the oil and 2 tablespoons lime juice together
with salt and pepper. Just before serving, pour the dressing over the
salad and toss gently to combine.

4 Slice the lamb and serve with watermelon salad.

Greek lamb with watermelon salad

Feta and spinach gozleme

Feta and spinach gozleme

makes 4

3¼ cups plain flour, sifted
2 teaspoons salt
⅓ cup olive oil
360ml lukewarm water
olive oil cooking spray
lemon wedges, to serve

Filling
1 tablespoon olive oil
1 large brown onion, finely chopped
2 large garlic cloves, crushed
pinch cayenne pepper
¼ teaspoon sweet paprika
2 bunches English spinach, shredded
200g feta cheese, crumbled
50g tasty cheese, grated

1 Combine the flour and salt in a large bowl and make a well in the centre. Combine the oil and water and pour into the flour. Use a flat-bladed knife to stir until combined. Turn onto a well-floured surface and knead until smooth and elastic. Divide the dough into four balls. Place on a lightly floured tray, cover with plastic wrap and set aside to rest for 20 minutes.

2 For the filling, heat the oil in a large frying pan over medium heat. Add the onions and garlic and cook 3-4 minutes until softened but not coloured. Transfer to a bowl and set aside to cool. Add the cayenne pepper, paprika, English spinach, feta and tasty cheese, stir to combine.

3 Preheat a barbecue flat plate on high until hot. Roll one piece of dough on a lightly floured surface into a 3mm-thick, 20cm x 30cm rectangle. Pile one-quarter of the filling onto half of the dough. Fold over the dough and press lightly to seal. Repeat with remaining dough and filling.

4 Spray the top with olive oil. Reduce barbecue heat to medium-low. Place a piece of baking paper onto the flat plate, place two gozlemes, oil-side down, onto the baking paper and barbecue for 3-4 minutes until golden. Spray with oil, turn over and barbecue a further 3-5 minutes until golden. Cut into pieces and serve with lemon wedges.

I have always marvelled at the Turkish women who make these. My friend Naomi showed me how and now they make regular appearances at my barbecues.

Fish cakes with quick chilli lime dipping sauce

serves 4 as a starter

500g redfish, snapper or ling boneless fillets,
  skin removed, chopped
2 tablespoons red curry paste
1 tablespoon fish sauce
1 egg white
1 tablespoon cornflour
1/4 cup shredded coconut
40g snake or green beans, trimmed, thinly sliced
3 kaffir lime leaves, spines removed, finely shredded
2 tablespoons coriander leaves, chopped
vegetable oil, for shallow-frying

Quick chilli lime dipping sauce
1/2 cup roasted salted peanuts, chopped
1 red banana chilli, halved, seeds removed
1 small red chilli, roughly chopped
1 garlic clove, roughly chopped
1/4 cup grated palm sugar or brown sugar
2 limes, juiced

1 Combine fish, curry paste, fish sauce, egg white, cornflour and coconut in a food processor. Process until just combined. Transfer mixture to a bowl.

2 Stir in beans, lime leaves and coriander. Using wet hands, shape mixture into eight patties. Cover and refrigerate 30 minutes if time permits.

3 For the quick chilli lime dipping sauce, combine roasted peanuts, chillies and garlic in food processor and process until finely chopped; alternatively, pound in a mortar and pestle. Transfer mixture to a saucepan. Stir in the palm sugar, 1/4 cup lime juice and 1/4 cup water. Bring to the boil over medium heat. Reduce heat to low and simmer, uncovered, for 3-5 minutes or until thickened slightly. Cool.

4 Heat oil in a frying pan over medium-high heat. Cook fish cakes, in batches, for 2 minutes each side or until golden and cooked through. Serve fish cakes warm with quick chilli lime dipping sauce.

Leftover chilli lime dipping sauce will keep for 4 weeks in the fridge.

Fish cakes with quick chilli lime dipping sauce

Barbecue duck wontons

Barbecue duck wontons

makes 24

24 wonton wrappers
2 tablespoons peanut oil
1 barbecue duck
200g fresh shiitake mushrooms, thinly sliced
1/4 cup hoisin sauce (Lee Kum Kee brand)
1 tablespoon chilli stir-fry paste
1 telegraph cucumber, peeled, halved, seeds removed,
   cut into thin strips
1 bunch coriander leaves

1 Preheat oven to 190°C no fan/180°C fan-forced. Brush both sides of
12 wonton wrappers with oil. Ease into a 12 x 1/3-cup capacity muffin
pan. Bake for 8-10 minutes, or until golden and crisp. Transfer to
a wire rack to cool. Repeat with remaining wrappers and oil.

2 Meanwhile, discard the skin from the duck. Shred the meat.

3 Heat a wok over medium-high heat. Add 1 tablespoon oil and the
mushrooms, stir-fry for 2 minutes. Add the duck, hoisin sauce and
stir-fry paste. Stir-fry 1-2 minutes until duck is well coated.

4 Spoon the duck mixture into the wonton cups, top with cucumber
strips and coriander leaves. Serve warm or at room temperature.

You can cook the wontons up to 4 hours ahead. They are best filled with the duck mixture just before serving.

Chilli stir-fry paste is available in the Asian section of the supermarket. Alternatively, use chilli jam (see page 233).

Beef kofta

serves 4

2 small red onions
1 1/4 cups coriander leaves
1 long green chilli, halved, seeds removed
500g beef mince
1 teaspoon ground coriander
1 teaspoon ground cumin
1/2 lemon, juiced
1 cup Greek-style yoghurt
olive oil
4 flat bread, to serve

If you don't have a food processor, finely chop the coriander and chilli and grate the onion. Use your hands to mix really well.

1 Roughly chop 1 red onion, place in a food processor with 1/2 cup coriander leaves and chilli. Process until very finely chopped. Add mince, ground coriander and cumin, and season with salt and pepper. Use the pulse button to process until well combined.

2 Using wet hands, mould heaped tablespoons of mixture around eight metal skewers, squeezing the mixture tightly. Place on a tray lined with baking paper. Cover and refrigerate 30 minutes if time permits.

3 Thinly slice the remaining red onion and place on a microwave-safe plate. Pour over the lemon juice, cover and microwave for 45 seconds on High/100%. Remove the cover and set aside to cool.

4 Finely chop another 1/2 cup coriander and stir into the yoghurt. Cover and refrigerate until ready to serve.

5 Preheat a barbecue's flat and ridged plates to medium. Drizzle the skewers with oil, turning to coat all sides. Barbecue skewers on the heated flat plate for 10 minutes for medium, turning often, or until cooked to your liking.

6 Brush the flat bread with oil and cook on the heated ridged plate for 1-2 minutes each side until warmed through. Place the kofta on flat bread, top with onions, remaining coriander and drizzle with the yoghurt mixture to serve.

This is a great mid-week meal — quick, fresh and inexpensive. You can prepare steps 1 to 4 the night before and just quickly cook the skewers when you get home.

Beef kofta

Spring vegetable minestrone

Spring vegetable minestrone

serves 4

2 tablespoons olive oil
1 garlic clove, crushed
1 small red onion, finely chopped
1 tablespoon tomato paste
1 leek, thinly sliced, washed, dried
2 carrots, peeled, diced
2 inner stalks celery, thinly sliced
4 cups vegetable or chicken stock
150g fresh peas in the pod, shelled
1/4 small green cabbage, shredded
2 zucchini, thinly sliced
toasted sourdough, to serve

Gremolata
1 large lemon, rind finely grated
1/4 cup flat-leaf parsley leaves, finely chopped
1 garlic clove, crushed

1 Heat the oil in a large saucepan over medium heat. Add the garlic and onion, cook, stirring, for 3 minutes until soft. Add tomato paste and cook, stirring, for 1 minute.

2 Add the leek, carrot and celery, stir to coat. Pour in the stock and bring to the boil. Cover and simmer for 15 minutes.

3 Add peas, cabbage and zucchini and cook for 5-8 minutes or until peas are tender. Taste and season with salt and pepper.

4 For the gremolata, combine the lemon rind, parsley and garlic in a small bowl.

5 Ladle the soup into serving bowls, sprinkle with the gremolata and serve with toasted sourdough.

Pumpkin, roasted hazelnut and feta salad

serves 10

1 cup hazelnuts
1.5kg butternut pumpkin,
 cut into 3cm pieces
olive oil cooking spray
175g marinated Persian feta cheese,
 drained

Honey and balsamic dressing
1/4 cup honey
2 tablespoons balsamic vinegar
1 tablespoon olive oil

1 Preheat oven to 240°C no fan/230°C fan-forced. While the oven is heating, place hazelnuts onto a baking tray, roast 10-15 minutes until skins crack and hazelnuts are roasted. Transfer to a clean tea towel, wrap to secure. Rub hazelnuts in tea towel to remove skins. Chop hazelnuts and set aside.

2 Line a large roasting pan with non-stick baking paper. Arrange the pumpkin in pan, spray with oil and season with salt and pepper. Roast, turning once, for 15 minutes or until golden brown and tender. Cool to room temperature.

3 For the honey and balsamic dressing, place all the ingredients and salt and pepper in a screw-top jar and shake well to combine. Remove lid. Microwave on High/100% for 10 seconds or until honey is melted. Shake until well combined.

4 Combine pumpkin, hazelnuts and feta on a serving platter, drizzle with dressing and serve.

Cos salad

serves 8

1 cup pine nuts
2 cos lettuces, leaves separated,
 washed
8 green onions, thinly sliced
3/4 cup fresh dill, roughly chopped

Dressing
1/2 cup extra virgin olive oil
2 1/2 tablespoons red wine vinegar
1 teaspoon caster sugar

1 Place pine nuts into a frying pan. Cook over medium-high heat, shaking the pan, for 5 minutes or until golden. Set aside to cool.

2 For the dressing, place all the ingredients and salt and pepper in a screw-top jar and shake well to combine.

3 Pat the lettuce leaves dry with paper towel. Place three or four leaves at a time on top of each other and finely shred. Place lettuce into a serving bowl. Add green onions, dill and toasted pine nuts and toss to combine. Just before serving, pour the dressing over the salad. Toss gently and serve.

This dish is from the Greek island of Cos. If I had to name my favourite salad this would be it. I make it all the time and I know you will too after you try it.

Front to back: Pumpkin, roasted hazelnut and feta salad; and Cos salad

Barbecued pork loin with roasted pears and potatoes

Barbecued pork loin with roasted pears and potatoes

serves 10

2.5-3kg rolled pork loin
2 tablespoons olive oil
1$^1/_2$ tablespoons fine table salt ◄ ·

Roasted pears and potatoes
1kg sebago potatoes, peeled, cut into 5cm pieces
4 beurre bosc pears, quartered, cored
40g butter, melted
2 tablespoons olive oil
2 tablespoons honey
2 teaspoons ground nutmeg

1 Preheat all the burners on the barbecue on high heat. Pat pork rind dry with paper towel. Rub oil all over rind. Sprinkle well with salt. Place pork on a wire rack in a large roasting pan. Pour enough water into the pan to cover the base.

2 Turn the burners under the flat plate off. Place roasting pan onto the flat plate. Close the barbecue hood and barbecue for 1$^1/_2$-2 hours, adding more water to the roasting pan every 30 minutes or until the crackling is golden and crisp and pork juices run clear when tested with a skewer. Turn all the burners off and allow pork to stand for 15 minutes before carving.

3 Meanwhile, preheat oven to 230°C no fan/220°C fan-forced. Place potatoes in a large saucepan. Cover with cold water. Bring to the boil, covered, over high heat. Reduce heat to medium. Partially cover saucepan and simmer for 15 minutes or until potatoes are just tender when pierced with a knife. Drain potatoes well.

4 Arrange the potatoes and pears in a large roasting pan. Combine the butter, oil, honey and nutmeg and spoon over the potatoes and pears, and turn to coat. Roast for 20-25 minutes, turning occasionally until golden and tender. Serve with pork.

Fine table salt produces a crisper crackling.

The intense dry heat of the barbecue produces the most sensational pork. If you don't have a barbecue, roast the pork in the oven for 30 minutes on 230°C no fan/ 220°C fan-forced then 35 minutes per kilo on 180°C no fan/ 170°C fan-forced.

Baked ricotta

serves 10

500g fresh ricotta cheese
2 tablespoons extra virgin olive oil
1 small red chilli, seeds removed, finely chopped
1 tablespoon fresh thyme leaves
lavoche, olives, sliced avocado, prosciutto
  and char-grilled vegetables, to serve

1 Carefully place the ricotta in a sieve over a bowl, cover loosely with paper towel and refrigerate 2 hours or overnight if time permits.

2 Preheat oven to 190°C no fan/180°C fan-forced. Lightly grease a shallow baking dish; lift the ricotta into the dish. Combine the oil, chilli, thyme and salt and pepper in a bowl and spoon mixture over the ricotta. Bake for 20 minutes or until edges are golden. Reduce the oven to 160°C no fan/150°C fan-forced, baste ricotta with hot oil mixture and bake for a further 30 minutes. Allow ricotta to cool to room temperature.

3 Store in an airtight container in the fridge for up to 8 days.

 You might look at this and wonder why it's included — it's not a main meal (well, occasionally for me it is). On weekends after eating all day or on balmy nights when I'm not really hungry, I sit down with a wedge of this and bits and pieces from the fridge and enjoy a healthy, high-protein meal. It can also double as a starter before a barbie.

Baked ricotta

Barbecued barramundi with balsamic roasted beetroot

Barbecued barramundi with balsamic roasted beetroot

serves 4

4 x 200g fillets barramundi, skin on
olive oil
150g baby rocket leaves
1/2 cup pecans, chopped

Balsamic roasted beetroot
2 tablespoons balsamic vinegar
2 large oranges, juiced
2 tablespoons brown sugar
1 tablespoon olive oil
6 medium beetroot

1 Preheat oven to 230°C no fan/220°C fan-forced. For the balsamic roasted beetroot, combine the vinegar, 1/3 cup orange juice, sugar, oil, and salt and pepper in a jug. Whisk to combine. Trim beetroot stalks, leaving 3cm attached. Gently scrub beetroot (don't peel). Pat dry with paper towel.

2 Place beetroot in a roasting pan in a single layer, pour the balsamic mixture over and turn to coat. Cover with foil. Roast for 1 hour or until just tender. Cut beetroot into quarters. Set aside to cool.

3 Heat a barbecue plate or frying pan over medium-high. Drizzle the barramundi with oil and season with salt and pepper. Cook, skin side down, for 4 minutes, pressing the fish down to crisp up the skin. Turn and cook a further 3-4 minutes or until just cooked through.

4 Combine the rocket, pecans and beetroot in a bowl; toss gently to combine. Pile onto serving plates, top with fish and spoon over beetroot pan juices. Serve.

Fresh beetroot are well worth the effort. They are in season from July to November but you can get them all year round. If you're short on time, use canned beetroot. Simmer the balsamic mixture until it's reduced by half, and use as the dressing.

Warm chicken, avocado and orange tahini salad

serves 4

1 tablespoon olive oil
600g chicken breast fillets
1 continental cucumber, halved lengthways,
  seeds removed
150g mixed salad leaves
3 oranges, peeled, segmented
2 avocados, halved, stones removed, peeled,
  thinly sliced crossways
1 tablespoon sesame seeds, toasted

Tahini dressing
1/4 cup extra virgin olive oil
1 orange, juiced
1 teaspoon brown sugar
1 teaspoon Dijon mustard
1 tablespoon tahini

Tahini is ground sesame seed paste. The fresh variety from health food stores is far better than the bottled one from the supermarket.

1 Heat oil in a large non-stick frying pan over medium heat. Add the chicken and cook for 5 minutes each side or until cooked through. Transfer to a plate, cover and set aside for 5 minutes to rest, then thinly slice.

2 Thinly slice the cucumber and place into a large bowl. Add the salad leaves, orange segments, avocado and warm chicken.

3 For the dressing, place all the ingredients and salt and pepper in a screw-top jar and shake until well combined.

4 Pour the dressing over the salad, add the sesame seeds and toss gently to combine. Serve.

Warm chicken, avocado and orange tahini salad

Spinach and ricotta omelette

Spinach and ricotta omelette

serves 2

1 tablespoon olive oil
1/2 bunch English spinach, shredded
2 green onions, thinly sliced
2 tablespoons flat-leaf parsley leaves, chopped
1 tablespoon butter
4 fresh free-range eggs, at room temperature
200g fresh ricotta cheese
toasted and buttered grain bread, to serve

1 Heat oil in a 20cm heavy-based frying pan (preferably non-stick with shallow sides so omelette will slide out easily), over medium-high heat. Add spinach, green onions and parsley and toss until spinach just wilts. Remove to a plate. Wash and dry the pan.

2 Reheat the pan over medium-high heat until just warm. Add half the butter. Tilt frying pan back and forth until the butter is sizzling.

3 Crack 2 eggs into a jug. Use a fork to beat eggs until the egg runs in a thin stream when you lift the fork out of the mixture. Pour into frying pan, tilting to cover base with egg. Using a wooden spoon, drag cooked egg from outer edge into centre. Tilt pan to allow uncooked egg to come in contact with pan.

4 Arrange half the spinach mixture over one-half of the omelette and crumble over half the ricotta. Fold the omelette over the filling and cook 1-2 minutes until warmed through. Slide onto hot toast. Season with salt and pepper. Repeat with remaining eggs, spinach mixture and ricotta to make another omelette.

High protein, low carbohydrate meals are really good options a few times a week. This is delicious, filling and healthy. Drop the bread and serve with a salad for an even lower carb meal!

Orange sweet potato, labne and rocket salad

serves 4

500g Greek-style yoghurt or purchased labne
1 bunch oregano, leaves removed
1 bunch flat-leaf parsley, leaves removed
1 cup walnuts
2 tablespoons icing sugar
1 teaspoon ground nutmeg
1/4 teaspoon cayenne pepper
1.25kg orange sweet potato, peeled, cut into 5cm pieces
2 tablespoons olive oil
150g baby rocket leaves
12 slices prosciutto, roughly chopped
1/3 cup vinaigrette (see page 237)
crusty bread, to serve

1 To make the labne, line a sieve with a piece of muslin or a clean new Chux cloth, then place over a bowl. Spoon the yoghurt into the lined sieve. Fold the muslin or cloth over the yoghurt, cover and stand in the fridge for 24 hours.

2 Finely chop the oregano and parsley and spread on a plate. Remove the yoghurt from the muslin or cloth, discard the liquid. Drop spoonfuls of yoghurt into the herbs and roll to coat. Use immediately or place into an airtight container, cover with olive oil and refrigerate for up to 1 week.

3 Preheat oven 200°C no fan/180°C fan-forced. Line a baking tray with baking paper. Place the walnuts in a sieve and rinse under cold water. Place in a single layer on the tray. Combine the icing sugar, nutmeg and cayenne pepper and sift over the walnuts, turning to coat both sides. Bake for 8-10 minutes or until caramelised. Set aside to cool, increase oven 240°C no fan/220°C fan-forced.

4 Arrange the sweet potato on a tray lined with baking paper. Drizzle with olive oil and season with salt and pepper, then turn to coat. Roast for 20-30 minutes, turning occasionally, until golden and tender. Set aside to cool for 15 minutes.

5 Arrange the rocket, prosciutto, walnuts and sweet potato on a large platter. Add the labne, drizzle with dressing, season with salt and pepper and serve with crusty bread.

Labne is a mild soft cheese, popular in the Middle East. It's really cheap and easy to make yourself from thick Greek yoghurt but can be bought from delis and cheese shops.

Orange sweet potato, labne and rocket salad

The best fish and chips

The best fish and chips

serves 4

1½ cups self-raising flour
300ml ice-cold beer or soda water
700g bream or flathead fillets, skin on
peanut oil, for deep-frying
twice-fried chips (see page 229), to serve
lemon, to serve

Tartare sauce
2 egg yolks
½ small lemon, juiced
½ teaspoon Tabasco sauce
100ml olive oil
2 gherkins, finely chopped
2 tablespoons flat-leaf parsley leaves, chopped
2 tablespoons capers, drained, chopped

1 For the tartare sauce, combine the egg yolks, 1 tablespoon lemon juice and Tabasco in a small food processor. Process until mixture starts to thicken. With the motor running, gradually drizzle in the oil in a thin steady stream until all the oil is incorporated. Transfer mayonnaise to a bowl, stir in gherkins, parsley, and capers, season with salt and pepper. Refrigerate until ready to serve.

2 Sift the flour and a pinch of salt into a bowl and make a well in the centre. Add beer or soda water. Stir gently with a wooden spoon to form a smooth batter: it should be the consistency of thickened cream.

3 Preheat oven to 170°C no fan/160°C fan-forced. Pour enough oil into a large, deep, heavy-based saucepan, wok or deep-fryer so it is one-third full. Heat over medium-high heat until hot.

4 Carefully cut each fish fillet down the centre to form two long thin fillets. Discard bones. Dip each fillet into batter, allow excess batter to drain away. Lower fish into oil, cook 2-3 pieces at a time for 3-4 minutes or until batter is crisp and golden. Remove to a wire rack to drain. Keep warm in oven on the rack while cooking remaining fish. Season with salt and pepper.

5 Serve with tartare sauce, twice-fried chips and lemon.

The sugar in the beer gives this batter its lovely golden colour.

The base for tartare sauce is mayonnaise. Homemade mayonnaise really is worth it, if you have the time — there are no preservatives or additives. If time doesn't permit, use 3/4 cup of whole egg mayonnaise.

Barbecued prawns with tzatziki and tabouli

serves 4

24 (about 1kg) king green prawns,
   peeled with tails intact, deveined
olive oil

Tzatziki
2 large Lebanese cucumbers, peeled, halved lengthways
1 teaspoon sea salt
500g Greek-style yoghurt
1/3 cup fresh mint leaves, chopped
2 small garlic cloves, crushed

Tabouli
1 cup burghul
3 ripe tomatoes, halved
2 bunches (3 cups) flat-leaf parsley leaves, chopped
2 bunches (1½ cups) fresh mint leaves, chopped
4 green onions, finely chopped
2 lemons, juiced
1/4 cup extra virgin olive oil

1 For the tzatziki, use a teaspoon to scrape the seeds from the cucumber halves. Coarsely grate the cucumber into a glass or ceramic bowl and sprinkle with salt. Cover and allow to stand for 30 minutes. Squeeze the excess moisture from the cucumber. Discard the liquid. Combine the yoghurt, mint, garlic, cucumber and season with pepper. Cover and refrigerate for 2 hours.

2 For the tabouli, place the burghul in a large bowl. Squeeze the tomato seeds and juice over the burghul, then cover and stand for 15 minutes. Dice the tomatoes and add to the burghul with the parsley, mint, green onions, 1/3 cup lemon juice and olive oil. Season with salt and pepper, and toss gently to combine.

3 Carefully thread the prawns onto 24 pre-soaked wooden skewers. Place on a plate and drizzle with olive oil; season with salt and pepper.

4 Preheat a barbecue plate on medium-high, barbecue the prawns for 2-3 minutes on each side or until they change colour and are just cooked through. Serve with tzatziki and tabouli.

Barbecued prawns with tzatziki and tabouli

Fresh inspirations

Schnitzel with apple and mint sauce

Peel and dice golden delicious apples. Microwave on high until tender. Add a spoonful of mint jelly and process or blend until smooth (sweeten with a little sugar if needed). Serve with pan-fried pork schnitzel.

Cheesy lamb rissoles

Grate carrot, zucchini and orange sweet potato, and add to lamb mince with grated cheese. Shape mixture into rissoles and pan-fry or barbecue until cooked through. Serve with tabouli (see page 126).

Mushroom gnocchi

Sauté chopped onion, garlic and sliced mushrooms in plenty of olive oil until tender. Toss over cooked gnocchi with lots of grated parmesan cheese. Season with salt and pepper and serve.

10-minute pumpkin curry

Peel and dice butternut pumpkin. Place on a plate and microwave until almost tender. Sauté onion in a little oil until soft, add red, green or yellow curry paste and stock. Add the pumpkin and a handful of green beans and simmer until tender.

Deli spaghetti

Warm chopped antipasti ingredients like artichokes, capsicum, eggplant and semi-dried tomatoes in olive oil. Squeeze over lemon juice and toss through cooked spaghetti.

Pan-fried fish with warm sesame slaw

Sauté shredded red and green cabbage with grated carrot and chopped green onions until just wilted. Add a dollop of thick yoghurt and toasted sesame seeds and toss to combine. Serve with pan-fried fish.

Lemongrass chicken kebabs

Combine chicken mince with loads of chopped fresh herbs, a handful of fresh breadcrumbs and a little sweet chilli sauce. Mould spoonfuls around sticks of lemongrass and barbecue or grill until golden and cooked through.

Macadamia crusted fish

Beat butter, garlic, chopped herbs and finely chopped macadamia nuts together, spread over both sides of white fish fillets. Wrap the fish with bacon or prosciutto and pan-fry until golden and cooked through. Serve with lemon-scented broccoli (see page 244).

Ginger and lime glazed steak

Soften a little ginger and lime marmalade in the microwave and brush over rump steak. Barbecue or pan-fry and serve with cucumber and radish salad (see page 20).

Lemon and bay leaf chicken

Skewer cubes of chicken with wedges of lemon and fresh bay leaves. Brush with olive oil and barbecue or grill until just cooked through. Serve with a dollop of tzatziki (see page 126) and orange mustard carrots (see page 246).

10-minute laksa

Fry laksa paste until aromatic. Add coconut milk and stock and bring to the boil, add shredded cooked chicken, carrot, cabbage and bean sprouts and simmer until warmed through. Serve with a squeeze of lime juice and sprinkle of grated palm sugar.

Spicy egg burger

Brush large flat mushrooms with olive oil. Barbecue mushrooms, hot pancetta and an egg and serve on a toasted hamburger bun with shredded lettuce and a dollop of chilli jam (see page 233).

Fabulous

My fondest memories of growing up are of walking into the family home to the aroma of freshly baked cakes or biscuits. The sweet memories always make me smile. I guess this is where I get my love for baking. Though I am well known for cooking up a Swiss roll, fudge brownies, lime coconut cakes or blueberry pancakes and three savouries in 20 minutes on *Ready Steady Cook*, I understand not everyone is as confident when it comes to desserts. I have included the tips you'll need to reproduce my recipes perfectly every time. As a general rule, most baking requires no oven fan. When a recipe gives good results with the fan on, I have given both oven temperatures. Enjoy and embrace these recipes!

Janelle's chocolate brownies and marshmallow hot chocolate

makes 24 brownies (makes 4 hot chocolates)

200g good-quality dark chocolate (like Plaistowe or Club), chopped
200g butter, chopped
$1/3$ cup cocoa powder
$1^1/2$ cups caster sugar
3 eggs, lightly beaten
$1/2$ cup plain flour
$1/4$ cup self-raising flour
200g good-quality white or milk chocolate, chopped
1 cup walnuts, chopped

Marshmallow hot chocolate
3 cups milk
150g good-quality dark chocolate, finely chopped
24 (100g) white marshmallows

1 Preheat oven to 180°C no fan. Grease and line 3cm-deep, 16cm x 26cm (base) slab pan with baking paper, allowing a 2cm overhang at both long ends (you can then lift the brownies out of the pan).

2 Place the dark chocolate and butter in a heatproof, microwave-safe bowl. Microwave, uncovered, for 2 minutes on High/100%, stirring every minute with a metal spoon until smooth.

3 Stir cocoa powder into the warm chocolate mixture until cocoa dissolves. Stir in sugar, then eggs. Mix well. Sift the flours together over the chocolate mixture, then stir to combine. Stir in the white or milk chocolate and walnuts. Spread mixture into prepared pan.

4 Bake brownie for 35-40 minutes or until a skewer inserted comes out with moist crumbs sticking. Cool completely in the pan. Cut into squares.

5 For the marshmallow hot chocolate, pour boiling water into four, heatproof, microwave-safe glasses. Meanwhile, place milk into a heatproof, microwave-safe jug; microwave, uncovered on High/100% for 3-4 minutes or until milk just comes to the boil. Pour the water out of the glasses, then spoon the chocolate evenly into the base of each glass. Pour over the milk and top each with marshmallows. Microwave, uncovered on High/100% for 40 seconds.

Janelle's chocolate brownies and marshmallow hot chocolate

Coconut cake with passionfruit glaze

Coconut cake with passionfruit glaze

serves 10

2¹/₃ cups desiccated coconut
1²/₃ cups caster sugar
2¹/₂ cups self-raising flour, sifted
2²/₃ cups coconut milk
2 eggs, lightly beaten

Passionfruit glaze
1¹/₂ cups icing sugar
2 fresh passionfruit, halved

1 Preheat oven to 170°C no fan. Grease a 2-litre Gugelhopf pan.

2 Combine coconut, sugar and flour in a large bowl. Add coconut milk and eggs and stir until well combined. Spoon mixture into prepared pan. Smooth the top.

3 Bake cake for 1 hour or until a skewer inserted into the centre comes out clean. Stand for 10 minutes in the pan before turning onto a wire rack to cool.

4 For the passionfruit glaze, sift icing sugar into a microwave-safe heatproof bowl, add 1¹/₂ tablespoons passionfruit pulp, stirring to form a very thick paste. Microwave, uncovered, for 30-40 seconds on High/100% cr until warm and runny.

5 Pour the warm glaze over the cake and allow to set before serving.

If you don't have a Gugelhopf pan, you can cook this cake in a 23cm springform cake pan for the same amount of time.

This method is the same for all icings. It ensures the icing will stick to the cake.

This cake combines two of my favourite ingredients — coconut and passionfruit. It's deliciously moist and just melts in your mouth.

These little cakes are as light as a feather. As kids we loved making them. They keep unfilled for a week in an airtight container at room temperature. But they never seemed to last that long in our household.

Jelly cakes

makes 40

2 x 85g packet jelly crystals of your choice (I used port wine)
4 cups desiccated coconut
300ml double cream

Cakes
3 tablespoons cornflour
1/4 cup plain flour
1/4 cup self-raising flour
3 x 59g eggs, at room temperature
1/2 cup caster sugar

1 Preheat oven to 180°C no fan. Grease two 30ml capacity mini muffin pans.

2 For the cakes, sift cornflour and plain and self-raising flours with a pinch of salt together three times to aerate. Using an electric mixer, beat eggs and sugar in a large bowl on high speed for 5 minutes, or until the mixture is thick and pale.

3 Sift flour mixture again over egg mixture, and gently fold until just combined. Spoon mixture into the muffin holes so they are two-thirds full. Bake for 12-14 minutes or until cakes have shrunk away from the sides slightly and spring back when gently touched. Remove from the pans while hot (or they will stick). Repeat with remaining mixture until all the cakes are baked.

4 Prepare jelly in a deep large bowl following packet instructions. Refrigerate 1 hour or until thick but not set (if jelly is too thin the cakes will fall apart). Place 5 cakes at a time into the jelly, turn to coat, allow to stand 2 minutes in jelly until they soften slightly, roll in coconut, place onto a wire rack for 1 hour to set. Re-dip the cakes in the jelly and coat in coconut again. Allow to set 1 hour.

5 Using a serrated knife, carefully cut cakes in half. Top each base with 1 teaspoon cream, sandwich halves together. Serve.

Jelly cakes

From left to right: CWA scones; Strawberry and lime jam

CWA Scones

makes 20

4 cups self-raising flour, sifted
¹/₂ teaspoon salt
1 cup pouring cream
375ml-400ml milk
double cream and strawberry and lime jam (see page 208),
  to serve

If you can't find
pouring cream,
thickened cream
will also work.

1 Preheat oven to 250°C no fan/230°C fan-forced. Lightly grease large flat oven tray.

2 Combine flour and salt in a large bowl. Add cream and 375ml milk. Use a flat-bladed knife to stir to a soft dough adding more milk if necessary. Turn onto a lightly floured surface and knead gently until dough comes together.

3 Press dough out to 2cm-thick. Using a 5.5cm round scone cutter, cut as many scones from dough as possible. Press dough scraps together gently, rolling it 2.5cm-thick and cut more scones. Repeat rolling the dough 5mm thicker each time until you have used all the dough. Place onto tray just touching each other.

4 Bake 12-15 minutes until golden and well risen. Serve hot with cream and jam.

I was invited to be a guest during the judging of the NSW state baking championships. What an honour. I watched these scones being made; and not only are they easy, they are the lightest, most delicious scones I have ever tasted (and believe me, I'm a Devonshire tea-lover).

Baklava ice-cream loaf

serves 6

$^1/_2$ cup walnuts
$^1/_2$ cup slivered almonds
$^1/_2$ cup pistachio kernels
2 teaspoons ground cinnamon
$^1/_4$ cup caster sugar
2 litres good-quality vanilla ice-cream
   (Blue Ribbon or Peters Buttermilk brand)

Honey-poached figs
$^3/_4$ cup honey
1 teaspoon ground cinnamon
375g dried figs

1 Grease and line a 6.5cm-deep, 11cm x 21cm (base) loaf pan, allowing a 2cm overhang on both long sides.

2 Preheat oven to 200°C no fan/190°C fan-forced. Spread nuts on a baking tray. Bake for 8-10 minutes or until toasted. Set aside to cool.

3 Roughly chop nuts and place into a bowl. Add cinnamon and sugar, mix well. Stand ice-cream at room temperature to soften slightly. Do not melt.

4 Spoon one-third of the ice-cream into the base of prepared pan. Sprinkle with one-third of nut mixture. Repeat the layers twice. Press to secure. Cover with plastic wrap and foil. Freeze for 6 hours or overnight if time permits.

5 For the honey-poached figs, combine honey, cinnamon and 1 cup water in a saucepan and bring to the boil over medium-high heat. Reduce heat and simmer for 10 minutes. Add the figs. Simmer, uncovered, for 15 minutes or until figs are plump and tender. Set aside to cool to room temperature.

6 Serve slices of ice-cream with honey-poached figs.

Make sure your spices are fresh. Old or stale spices can ruin a dish.

I really love this dessert as it can be made well ahead when entertaining. If there are leftovers the ice-cream is delicious scooped into waffle cones and the figs are scrumptious spooned over yoghurt and muesli for breakfast.

Baklava ice-cream loaf

Tiramisu cheesecake

Tiramisu cheesecake

serves 8

3/4 cup strong brewed espresso coffee
1/4 cup Kahlua liqueur
14 thin sponge finger biscuits
375g cream cheese, at room temperature, chopped
3/4 cup caster sugar
1 teaspoon vanilla bean paste
3 eggs, at room temperature
250g carton sour cream
250g mascarpone (Southcape brand)

Topping
1 egg white
2 tablespoons caster sugar
200ml double cream
80g milk chocolate, grated

1 Preheat oven to 160°C no fan. Line base and sides of a 23cm (base) springform pan with baking paper.

2 Combine coffee and Kahlua in a shallow dish. Quickly dip the biscuits, one at a time, into coffee mixture. Arrange over base of prepared pan, cutting the biscuits where necessary so the base is completely covered.

3 Using an electric mixer, beat cream cheese, sugar and vanilla until creamy and smooth. Add eggs, one at a time, beating well after each addition. Gently fold in sour cream and mascarpone until just combined. Pour cheesecake mixture over the base. Place onto a baking tray.

4 Bake cheesecake for 50-60 minutes or until a skewer inserted into the centre comes out clean (the centre should still wobble slightly). Turn the oven off and leave the door ajar for 3-4 hours or until cheesecake is cool.

5 For the topping, use an electric mixer to beat the egg white to soft peaks. Add the sugar and beat until well combined. Beat the cream with a balloon whisk to soft peaks; fold in the egg white mixture. Spoon over the cheesecake and sprinkle with chocolate. Cut with a warm knife to serve.

The centre of a baked cheesecake should still be wobbly. Don't be tempted to cook for longer as the cheesecake will crack on cooling.

Condensed milk choc chip biscuits

makes 40

250g butter, softened, chopped
1/2 cup caster sugar
1/2 x 395g can sweetened condensed milk
2 1/2 cups plain flour
3 1/2 teaspoons baking powder
375g choc bits or chopped milk
    chocolate

1 Preheat oven to 180°C no fan/170°C fan-forced. Line four baking trays with baking paper.

2 Using an electric mixer, beat butter, sugar and condensed milk until pale and creamy. Sift flour and baking powder together over the butter mixture and mix until the dough almost comes together. Add chocolate and stir until well distributed.

3 Roll heaped tablespoons of mixture into balls and place onto baking trays, allowing a little room for spreading. Flatten slightly with fingertips or a fork.

4 Bake two trays at a time for 9-12 minutes until light golden. Stand 5 minutes on trays before transferring biscuits to a wire rack to cool.

Janelle's peanut butter cookies

makes 24

375g jar peanut butter (Kraft brand)
1 cup caster sugar
1 egg
200g white chocolate, roughly chopped

1 Preheat oven to 180°C no fan/170°C fan-forced. Line two baking trays with baking paper.

2 Combine peanut butter, sugar and egg in a bowl, stir with a wooden spoon until the mixture thickens (keep stirring until it does). Add chocolate and stir until well distributed.

3 Roll tablespoons of mixture into balls and place on prepared trays, flatten with fingertips to about 1cm thick.

4 Bake one tray of cookies at a time for 12-15 minutes or until light golden and a little darker around the edges (you can smell when they are ready). Allow to cool on trays for 10 minutes then transfer to a wire rack to cool completely.

Variation For macadamia white chocolate cookies, reduce the white chocolate to 100g and add 100g roughly chopped macadamia nuts.

 These are my all-time favourite cookies and I know you will love them too. Quick, easy and delicious!

From front to back: Janelle's peanut butter cookies; Condensed milk choc chip biscuits

Mum's big apple cake

Mum's big apple cake

serves 12

250g butter, at room temperature, chopped
1 cup caster sugar
1 teaspoon vanilla extract
4 eggs, at room temperature
2½ cups self-raising flour
½ cup milk
1 tablespoon boiling water
4 Granny Smith apples

Topping
1 teaspoon ground cinnamon
2 tablespoons caster sugar
30g butter, chilled, finely chopped

1 Preheat oven to 180°C no fan. Grease and line an 8cm-deep, 22cm (base) square cake pan with baking paper, allowing a 3cm overhang at two opposite sides.

2 Using an electric mixer, beat the butter, sugar and vanilla until pale and creamy. Add eggs, one at a time, beating well after each addition. Sift flour over butter mixture and stir gently to combine. Stir in milk followed by the water. Spread mixture into prepared pan and smooth the surface.

3 Peel and grate apples and squeeze with your hands to remove excess moisture. Sprinkle the apple over the cake batter.

4 For the topping, combine cinnamon and sugar and sprinkle over the apples. Dot butter over top.

5 Bake cake for 1 hour or until a skewer inserted into the centre comes out clean. Stand for 10 minutes in the pan. Carefully lift the cake out of the pan and set aside to cool.

Mum gave me her treasured handwritten recipe book (which you can see here and on the contents page), and through its well-thumbed pages I hope to continue her loving culinary tradition for years to come.

This cake is my mum's specialty. When we were kids, allowing it to cool was always a challenge!

Foolproof chocolate caramel slice

makes 18

1 cup plain flour
1/2 cup brown sugar
1/2 cup desiccated coconut
125g butter, melted

Caramel filling
395g can sweetened condensed milk
2 tablespoons golden syrup
50g butter, chopped

Chocolate topping
200g good-quality dark chocolate (like Plaistowe or Club), chopped
1/4 cup pouring cream

1 Preheat oven to 180°C no fan. Line base and sides of a 3cm-deep, 16cm x 26cm slab pan with baking paper, allowing a 2cm overhang at both long sides.

2 Combine the flour, brown sugar and coconut in a bowl. Add butter and stir to combine. Press mixture over the base of the prepared pan. Bake for 10-15 minutes or until light golden.

3 For the caramel filling, combine the condensed milk, golden syrup and butter in an 2-litre capacity heatproof, microwave-safe bowl. Microwave, uncovered, for 3-4 minutes on High/100%, whisking every minute until light golden and thickened slightly. Pour the warm caramel over the warm base.

4 Bake slice a further 10-12 minutes or until the edges are deep golden. Set aside to cool 1 hour.

5 For the chocolate topping, place the chocolate and cream in a heatproof, microwave-safe bowl. Microwave, uncovered, in 1 minute bursts on High/100%, stirring after each minute with a metal spoon, until smooth.

6 Spread the chocolate over the room temperature caramel. Set aside until firm. Cut into squares using a warm knife.

Variation Add 1 cup chopped roasted hazelnuts to the caramel before pouring over the base in step 3.

I know most people have a recipe for caramel slice, but this method really is foolproof.

When I refer to heatproof, microwave-safe bowls or jugs, I use Pyrex.

Foolproof chocolate caramel slice

Meringues with lemon curd and raspberries

Meringues with lemon curd and raspberries

makes 30

4 x 59g free-range egg whites, at room temperature
pinch cream of tartar
1 cup caster sugar
250g fresh or frozen raspberries

Microwave lemon curd
3 eggs
2 egg yolks
3/4 cup caster sugar
1 lemon, rind finely grated
4 large lemons, juiced
125g butter, chilled, chopped

1 Preheat oven to 120°C no fan. Line two large baking trays with baking paper.

2 Using an electric mixer, beat the egg whites and cream of tartar on high speed until soft peaks form. Reduce the speed to medium-low. Add sugar, 1 tablespoon at a time, beating constantly until well combined. After adding the final spoonful of sugar, increase speed to high and beat for 2 minutes or until meringue is thick and glossy and sugar has dissolved.

3 Drop heaped tablespoons of meringue onto trays, allowing room for spreading. Using a teaspoon, make an indentation in the centre of each meringue. Place trays in oven, reduce oven to 100°C no fan and bake for 1¼ hours or until dry to touch. Turn off the oven and allow meringues to cool completely in the oven with the door ajar.

4 For the lemon curd, place eggs, egg yolks, sugar, and lemon rind in a 6-cup heatproof, microwave-safe bowl. Beat with balloon whisk until combined then add 3/4 cup lemon juice, whisking constantly. Add the butter. Microwave, uncovered, for 7-10 minutes on Medium/50%, whisking every minute until mixture just comes to the boil. Pour into sterilised jars, seal and label. Refrigerate until ready to use.

5 Spoon a small amount of lemon curd into the indentation on each meringue. Top with a raspberry and serve.

Variation For a passionfruit curd, replace the lemon juice with 3/4 cup fresh passionfruit pulp.

Lemon curd or butter has a reputation for being difficult. I promise this recipe works every time. Leftovers can be stored in a clean jar in the fridge for 2-3 weeks. I love it spread thickly on toasted crumpets.

Fill the meringues just before serving.

Banana walnut bread

serves 8

2 cups self-raising flour
1 teaspoon bicarbonate of soda
1 teaspoon ground nutmeg
1/2 cup brown sugar
3/4 cup walnuts, chopped
1 cup milk
2 eggs, lightly beaten
1 cup mashed banana
1 tablespoon raw sugar

1 Preheat oven to 180°C no fan. Grease 7cm-deep, 13.5cm x 24cm (base) loaf pan then line with baking paper, allowing 2cm overhang on both long sides.

2 Sift flour, bicarbonate of soda and nutmeg into a large bowl. Stir in sugar and walnuts. Combine milk, eggs and banana in a bowl and stir gently into the dry ingredients. Spoon mixture into prepared pan and smooth the surface. Sprinkle with the raw sugar.

3 Bake loaf for 45-50 minutes or until a skewer inserted into the centre comes out clean. Stand 5 minutes in the pan before lifting loaf onto a wire rack to cool.

4 Slice and serve, fresh or toasted, with butter or jam.

 You will need 2 large bananas for 1 cup of mashed banana — soft, overripe bananas are best. This loaf will keep for up to 7 days in an airtight container, and it freezes well.

Banana walnut bread

From left to right: Cinnamon-crusted macadamia nuts; Chilli caramel cashews

Cinnamon-crusted macadamia nuts

serves 10

2 egg whites, at room temperature
pinch sea salt
1/3 cup caster sugar
1 cup demerara sugar
2 tablespoons ground cinnamon
4 cups (580g) macadamia nuts

1 Preheat oven to 180°C no fan/160°C fan-forced. Line a large roasting pan with baking paper.

2 Using an electric mixer, beat egg whites and salt in a bowl until soft peaks form. Add caster sugar, 1 tablespoon at a time, beating constantly until well combined. Fold demerara sugar and cinnamon into meringue. Add macadamia nuts and stir until well coated. Spread mixture over base of prepared pan.

3 Bake for 10 minutes, then stir with a large metal spoon to break up mixture. Bake a further 20 minutes, stirring every 5-8 minutes or until cinnamon sugar crust feels dry (really important to stir otherwise the coating will fall off the nuts when cooled).

4 Cool nuts completely in pan. Break up and place in an airtight container. Serve with cocktails.

Chilli caramel cashews

serves 8

olive oil cooking spray
50g butter
1/2 cup honey
1 1/2 teaspoons salt flakes
1 teaspoon smoked paprika
1 teaspoon chilli powder
750g raw cashew nuts

1 Preheat oven to 200°C no fan/190°C fan-forced. Lightly grease a large flat baking tray.

2 Melt butter in a medium frying pan over medium heat. Add honey, salt, paprika, chilli powder and 1/4 cup water and bring to the boil. Add the cashew nuts and cook, stirring, for 2-3 minutes or until well coated.

3 Pour mixture onto the tray, carefully spreading out. Bake 5-10 minutes until firm to touch. Set aside to cool. Tap the tray on the bench to separate the nuts. Serve with cocktails.

When I was testing these recipes I took samples in to Channel 10 for an approval rating. The thumbs all went up as a must-include!

Delicious and
decadent, this
is one of the
yummiest
cheesecakes you
will ever eat. It
was developed
after a cooking
marathon with
a friend who
then baked it
for corporate
boxes during the
Wimbledon tennis
championships.

New York brownie cheesecake

serves 10

100g dark chocolate, chopped
100g butter, chopped
1^1/$_2$ tablespoons cocoa powder
^{1}/$_2$ cup caster sugar
1 egg, lightly beaten
^{1}/$_4$ cup plain flour
2 tablespoons self-raising flour
300ml double cream
2 tablespoons limoncello liqueur
cocoa powder, to serve

Filling
750g cream cheese, at room temperature, chopped
1 cup caster sugar
1 teaspoon vanilla extract
4 eggs, at room temperature
2 tablespoons plain flour
300g carton sour cream

1 Preheat oven to 180°C no fan. Grease and line the base and side of 23cm (base) springform pan with baking paper.

2 Combine chocolate and butter in a microwave-safe, heatproof bowl. Microwave, uncovered, for 2 minutes on High/100%. Stir until smooth. Whisk in cocoa powder until smooth. Stir in sugar, egg and flours. Spread mixture over base of prepared pan. Bake brownie base 15 minutes. Set aside 15 minutes. Reduce oven to 160°C no fan.

3 For the filling, use an electric mixer to beat the cream cheese, sugar and vanilla until just combined. Add the eggs, one at a time, beating well after each addition. Stir in the flour and sour cream until just combined. Pour over warm base and place on a baking tray.

4 Bake cheesecake for 1^1/$_4$-1^1/$_2$ hours or until a skewer inserted into the centre comes out clean (the centre should still wobble slightly). Turn oven off, leave the door ajar, and allow to cool completely in the oven. Refrigerate until chilled.

5 Place the cream and limoncello in a bowl, whisk gently until combined. Cut the cheesecake into wedges with a warm knife, dust with cocoa powder and serve with limoncello cream.

After baking
15 minutes, the
base will still
be a little soft.

New York brownie cheesecake

Shortbread

Shortbread

makes 32

250g butter, at room temperature
1/2 cup caster sugar
1 teaspoon vanilla extract
2 cups plain flour, sifted
1/3 cup white sugar
2 teaspoons ground cinnamon

1 Using an electric mixer, beat butter, caster sugar and vanilla until pale and creamy. Add the flour and stir until the dough comes together. Turn onto a lightly floured surface and knead gently until smooth. Cut the dough in half, press each piece of dough into a 2cm-thick round. Wrap in greaseproof paper and refrigerate until firm enough to roll out.

2 Roll the dough out until 1cm-thick. Using 5cm cutters, cut out shortbreads and place on a tray lined with baking paper. Place the trays in the freezer and chill for 10 minutes until firm (this helps shortbread hold its shape while baking). Press any unused dough together, re-roll and repeat.

3 Preheat oven to 170°C no fan/160°C fan-forced. Bake shortbread for 20-25 minutes or until light golden.

4 Combine the white sugar and cinnamon. Remove shortbread from the oven and stand 5 minutes on trays. While hot, brush with water and sprinkle or toss in cinnamon sugar. Serve warm or at room temperature.

Don't be tempted to wrap the dough in plastic. It will cause it to sweat.

White chocolate raspberry croissant cake

serves 6

Day-old croissants are best.

8 croissants, cut into four crossways
2 eggs
1/2 cup caster sugar
1/3 cup thickened cream
1/4 cup almond meal (ground almonds)
250g fresh or frozen raspberries
200g good-quality white chocolate, chopped
2 tablespoons flaked almonds
icing sugar, to serve
double cream or ice-cream, to serve

1 Lightly grease base and sides of a 6cm-deep, 20cm round springform cake pan.

2 Arrange half the croissants, cut-side up, in the prepared pan, making sure the base is completely covered. Combine the eggs, sugar, thickened cream and almond meal in a bowl. Use a fork to whisk until well combined. Pour half the egg mixture over the croissants. Stand for 10 minutes to allow the croissants to absorb some of the mixture.

3 Sprinkle over three-quarters of the raspberries and three-quarters of the white chocolate. Top with remaining croissants. Pour over remaining egg mixture and stand for 10 minutes.

4 Preheat oven and a baking tray to 180°C no fan/170°C fan-forced. Top with remaining raspberries and white chocolate, then sprinkle with the flaked almonds. Place cake pan on the hot baking tray and bake for 25-30 minutes or until golden. Stand cake for 10 minutes in the pan. Dust with icing sugar and serve warm with cream or ice-cream.

 Delicious, delicious are the only two words to describe this pudding/cake. Eat it while it's still warm (although it does reheat well).

White chocolate raspberry croissant cake

Roasted macadamia truffles

Roasted macadamia truffles

makes 36

125g roasted macadamia nuts
3/4 cup desiccated coconut
2/3 cup coconut cream
2 tablespoons Tia Maria or Kahlua liqueur
400g good-quality dark chocolate (Plaistowe or Club brand),
   broken into squares
1/2 cup cocoa powder, sifted

1 Preheat oven to 180°C no fan/170°C fan-forced. Line a baking tray with baking paper. Place the macadamia nuts on the tray and cook for 5-6 minutes or until warm. Set aside to cool, process until finely chopped.

2 Place coconut on the tray and cook in oven for 2-3 minutes or until toasted. Set aside to cool.

3 Combine the coconut cream, liqueur and chocolate in a medium heatproof bowl over simmering water. Stir with a metal spoon for 5-6 minutes or until the mixture is smooth; alternatively, microwave, uncovered, in 1-minute bursts on High/100%. Remove from the heat.

4 Add the macadamia nuts and coconut and stir until well combined. Refrigerate for 3 hours or until firm enough to roll into balls.

5 Place cocoa powder on a plate. Using 3 teaspoons of mixture per truffle, roll one at a time into a small ball and toss in cocoa powder to coat. Refrigerate until firm. Serve at room temperature.

Variation Replace the dark chocolate with white chocolate and coat in coconut.

Store unused coconut and nuts in the freezer to prevent them going stale.

Instead of buying chocolates I make these to take as a thank-you when I go to friends' homes for a meal. Homemade is so much better.

This cake is way too good to make just at Christmas time, and the fruit requires no soaking so it's dead easy! It will keep for weeks in an airtight container at room temperature.

Fig and raisin fruit cake

serves 16

1/2 cup brandy, dark rum or Kahlua
1/2 cup golden syrup
2/3 cup olive oil
200g dessert figs, chopped
150g pitted dates, chopped
200g raisins
150g sultanas
1 teaspoon ground nutmeg
1 teaspoon ground cinnamon
1 cup firmly packed brown sugar
3 eggs, at room temperature
1 1/4 cups plain flour
1/2 teaspoon baking powder

1 Preheat oven to 150°C no fan. Grease and line base and sides of a 7cm-deep, 19cm (base) square cake pan with baking paper.

2 Combine brandy, golden syrup and olive oil in a medium, heavy-based saucepan over medium heat. Heat for 5 minutes or until mixture just comes to the boil. Reduce heat to medium-low, add all the dried fruit, heat, without stirring, for 5 minutes or until the fruit is warm. Transfer mixture to a large bowl, stir in the nutmeg and cinnamon while warm. Set aside for 1 hour to cool.

3 Stir in brown sugar and eggs one at a time. Sift the flour and baking powder together over the fruit mixture and stir until just combined. Spoon mixture into prepared pan and smooth the surface.

4 Bake cake for 1 1/4-1 1/2 hours or until a skewer inserted into the centre comes out clean. Allow to cool completely in the pan. Decorate with fondant stars if desired.

To make fondant stars, roll a packet of white fondant out between two sheets of baking paper. Use various sizes of star-shaped cookie cutters to cut out stars. Attach coloured cachous to the stars with a little melted white chocolate. Allow to set before attaching to the cake with melted white chocolate.

Fig and raisin fruit cake

Rhubarb and strawberry refrigerator muffins

Rhubarb and strawberry refrigerator muffins

makes 18

4 cups plain flour
3$\frac{1}{2}$ teaspoons bicarbonate of soda
$\frac{1}{2}$ teaspoon salt
1$\frac{1}{3}$ cups brown sugar
2 cups processed bran cereal
2 eggs
$\frac{2}{3}$ cup canola or extra light olive oil
2 tablespoons golden syrup
2 cups milk
$\frac{2}{3}$ cup Greek-style yoghurt
250g (2 large stalks) rhubarb, trimmed, washed, diced
250g strawberries, hulled, diced
$\frac{1}{3}$ cup white sugar

Processed bran cereal is available from the health food aisle of the supermarket.

1 Sift flour, bicarbonate of soda and salt together into a large bowl. Stir in brown sugar and bran. Combine eggs, oil, golden syrup, milk, yoghurt and 1 cup cold water in a bowl. Whisk with a fork to combine. Pour into the dry ingredients and stir to combine. Fold in rhubarb and strawberries. Transfer to an airtight container. Cover. Refrigerate for at least 6 hours.

2 Preheat oven to 190°C no fan. Lightly grease six 180ml-capacity Texas muffin holes, alternatively line with paper cases.

3 Gently stir the muffin mixture, then spoon mixture into each muffin hole until three-quarters full. Sprinkle 1 teaspoon white sugar over each. Bake for 22-25 minutes or until a skewer inserted into the centre comes out clean. Repeat with remaining batter. Serve warm or at room temperature.

 It's great to keep a batch of this mixture in the fridge and bake up fresh muffins for a quick easy breakfast or after-school snack. It will keep for up to 10 days in the fridge.

This mud cake
has been baked
again and again
for family and
friends' wedding
cakes, nieces' and
nephews' birthday
cakes and is high
on the request list
when I go visiting.

My favourite mud cake

serves 8

300g good-quality dark chocolate (Plaistowe, Club or Dove brand)
200g butter, chopped
1/4 cup strong black espresso coffee
1/4 cup cocoa powder
1 teaspoon vanilla extract
1 cup caster sugar
3 eggs, lightly beaten
3/4 cup self-raising flour
thick cream, to serve

1 Preheat oven to 160°C no fan. Grease and line base and sides of
a 6cm-deep, 20cm (base) round cake pan.

2 Chop 200g of the chocolate. Place chopped chocolate, butter and
coffee in a heatproof, microwave-safe bowl. Microwave, uncovered,
for 2-3 minutes on High/100%, stirring every minute with a metal
spoon until smooth. Add cocoa while warm, whisk until smooth.

3 Whisk in vanilla, sugar and eggs. Sift flour over the chocolate
mixture and stir gently to combine. Roughly chop the remaining 100g
of chocolate.

4 Pour half the mixture into the prepared pan. Sprinkle half the
chocolate over the cake mixture. Pour remaining mixture over the
chocolate, top with remaining chocolate. Bake cake for 55-60 minutes
or until a skewer inserted into the centre has moist crumbs clinging.
Stand in pan to cool completely.

5 Use a warm knife to slice the cake, then serve with cream.

Variation You can replace the 100g dark chocolate with a chopped Mars
bar, Snickers bar or caramel chocolate. It is best to place these in
the freezer first so they are firm before you chop them.

This cake is
decadent and
borders on 'over
the top' when iced
(see page 199).
But, you guessed
it, I ice it more
often than not.

My favourite mud cake

From left to right: Rocky road trees; Bailey's fudge

Rocky road trees

makes 4

4 x 375g packets milk chocolate melts
4 x 100g packets white marshmallows
600g rose-flavoured Turkish delight
2 cups roasted salted peanuts,
   roughly chopped
ribbon, to decorate

1 Cut four 24cm squares from a sheet of flexible cardboard. Place onto a flat surface. Cut four 24cm squares of baking paper and place over each cardboard square. Staple the corners to secure. Holding one corner, roll cardboard to form a cone shape. Staple or tape the cone to secure.

2 Place one packet of milk chocolate melts into a heatproof bowl over a saucepan of simmering water. Stir with a metal spoon until melted; alternatively microwave, uncovered, in 1-minute bursts on Medium/50%. Stand the cone point-side down in a tall glass. Spoon 2-3 tablespoons melted chocolate into the point of the cone.

3 Chop one packet of marshmallows and 150g Turkish delight. Add to the remaining melted chocolate with 1/2 cup of peanuts, then stir to combine. Spoon mixture into the cone, pressing firmly to compact the rocky road. Repeat to make the remaining three trees. Refrigerate 2-3 hours or until set.

4 Carefully remove cardboard and paper. Decorate and serve.

Bailey's fudge

makes 20 pieces

395g can sweetened condensed milk
1 cup firmly packed brown sugar
125g butter, chopped
2 tablespoons liquid glucose
200g good-quality dark chocolate
   (Plaistowe or Club), finely chopped
3/4 cup pistachio kernels,
   roughly chopped
30ml Bailey's liqueur

1 Lightly grease base and sides of a 20cm (base) square cake pan. Line the base and sides with non-stick baking paper, allowing a 3cm overhang on all four sides.

2 Combine sweetened condensed milk, brown sugar, butter and glucose in a 2-litre heatproof, microwave-safe pyrex bowl. Microwave, uncovered, for 6-8 minutes on Medium-High/70% or until the mixture begins to boil, stirring every 2 minutes with a balloon whisk.

3 Microwave mixture for a further 3-4 minutes on Medium-High/70% or until the fudge is thick, golden and boils rapidly, stirring every minute with a wooden spoon. Very carefully place the bowl on a board and set aside for 1 minute or until the bubbles subside. Add chocolate and stir until the chocolate melts and the mixture is smooth. Stir in pistachios and liqueur.

4 Spread mixture evenly into the prepared pan. Set aside 3-4 hours or until firm. Remove from the pan, wrap in greaseproof or non-stick baking paper and store in an airtight container in the fridge. Cut into small pieces to serve.

Good for the hips
— well, not as
bad as you might
think! These are
so much fun to
make and so
delicious on a cold
winter's day with
the family. I am
confident you'll
make them more
than once.

Berry doughnuts

makes 30

1¼ cups plain flour
1 teaspoon instant dried yeast
½ cup caster sugar
pinch salt
1 egg
½ cup sour cream
20g butter, melted
fresh or frozen blueberries or raspberries
light olive oil or vegetable oil, for deep-frying
½ cup white sugar
1 tablespoon ground cinnamon

1 Combine flour, yeast, sugar and salt in bowl. Whisk egg and sour cream together until well combined. Stir into the flour mixture with the butter, mix to a firm dough.

Don't make the
doughnuts any
bigger than a
teaspoon. If
they're too big,
they won't cook
all the way to
the centre.

2 Using lightly floured hands, roll teaspoons of mixture into small balls and place onto a tray. Press one frozen berry into the centre of each ball and re-roll making sure the berry is completely covered in dough.

3 Half fill a saucepan or deep-fryer with oil and heat over medium heat until hot.

4 Combine the white sugar and cinnamon on a tray. Drop four to six doughnuts into the oil, and deep-fry for 3 minutes or until golden. Remove from the oil with a slotted spoon and roll in cinnamon sugar immediately. Repeat, until all the doughnuts are cooked, reheating the oil between batches if necessary. Serve hot with marshmallow hot chocolate (see page 134).

Berry doughnuts

Sticky date pudding with caramel sauce

Sticky date pudding with caramel sauce

serves 8

250g pitted dates, chopped
1¹/₂ cups boiling water
1 teaspoon bicarbonate of soda
125g butter, at room temperature, chopped
³/₄ cup brown sugar
1 teaspoon vanilla extract
2 eggs, at room temperature
2 cups self-raising flour, sifted
double cream, to serve (optional)

Caramel sauce
1¹/₂ cups white sugar
300ml carton thickened cream

1 Preheat oven to 180°C no fan. Grease and line base of a 7cm-deep, 22cm (base) round cake pan with baking paper.

2 Combine dates and boiling water in a saucepan over medium-high heat and bring to the boil. Cook, uncovered, 5 minutes until dates are soft and have almost absorbed all the water. Remove from heat, stir in bicarbonate of soda. Set aside for 20 minutes to cool.

3 Using an electric mixer, beat the butter, sugar and vanilla until pale and creamy. Add eggs, one at a time, beating well after each addition. Fold in the flour, then the date mixture. Spoon mixture into prepared pan.

4 Bake pudding for 40-45 minutes or until a skewer inserted into the centre comes out clean. Stand pudding in the pan for 10 minutes before turning onto a wire rack.

5 For the caramel sauce, pour the sugar into a clean, dry non-stick frying pan over medium heat. Cook, stirring occasionally with a wooden spoon until the sugar melts and turns deep golden. Remove pan from the heat, carefully pour in cream (sugar will crystalise). Return pan to medium-high heat, cook stirring constantly for 8 minutes to dissolve the sugar. Boil gently, without stirring, for 5 minutes to thicken slightly.

6 Cut or spoon warm pudding onto plates, pour over the sauce and serve with cream if desired.

Who doesn't love sticky date pudding? This is another recipe that can be made ahead and reheated. Warm the pudding in the microwave for 6-8 minutes on Medium/50% and the sauce for 3-4 minutes on High/100%.

Be patient with the caramel. The toffee will dissolve in the cream to produce the best caramel.

Olive oil raspberry cake

serves 10

4 eggs, at room temperature
2 cups caster sugar
1 teaspoon vanilla extract
1 cup extra light olive oil
1 cup apple or pear juice
3 cups plain flour
1 teaspoon baking powder
300g fresh or frozen raspberries
1 tablespoon icing sugar

Raspberry cream
300ml double cream
150g fresh or frozen raspberries

1 Preheat oven to 170°C no fan. Grease and line the base and sides of a 4cm-deep, 20cm x 29cm slab pan with baking paper, allowing a 2cm overhang at both long sides.

2 Using an electric mixer, beat eggs, caster sugar and vanilla in a large bowl on high speed for 3 minutes or until pale and thick. Stir in oil and apple juice. Sift flour and baking powder together over the egg mixture. Fold gently until combined.

3 Pour two-thirds of cake mixture into the prepared pan. Top with half the raspberries. Pour in remaining cake mixture. Top with remaining raspberries. Bake cake for 50-60 minutes or until a skewer inserted into the centre comes out clean. Stand cake in the pan for 10 minutes, then use the baking paper to carefully lift it out onto a wire rack to cool.

4 For the raspberry cream, whisk the cream in a large bowl until thick. Mash the raspberries with a fork and swirl through the cream.

5 Dust the cake with icing sugar just before serving with the raspberry cream.

Olive oil raspberry cake

Soft-centred chocolate puddings

Soft-centred chocolate puddings

serves 4

125g butter, softened
1/3 cup white sugar
200g good-quality dark chocolate (like Plaistowe or Club), chopped
3 eggs, at room temperature
2/3 cup caster sugar
1/4 cup self-raising flour
thickened cream, to serve (optional)

Chocolate fudge sauce
200g good-quality dark chocolate, chopped
1/3 cup thickened cream

1 Preheat oven to 180°C no fan. Using 1 tablespoon of the butter, lightly grease four 3/4-cup capacity ovenproof bowls. Sprinkle 1 tablespoon white sugar into each bowl and turn to coat.

2 Place chocolate and remaining 100g butter in a heatproof bowl over a saucepan of simmering water. Heat, stirring with a metal spoon, for 5 minutes or until smooth; alternatively, microwave, uncovered, on High/100% in 1-minute bursts. Remove from heat.

3 Using an electric mixer, beat eggs and caster sugar on high speed for 3 minutes until pale and thick. Stir in the warm chocolate mixture. Sift the flour over the mixture and stir gently to combine. Pour pudding mixture evenly into bowls; place on a tray. Bake for 20-25 minutes or until pudding tops are cracked.

4 Stand puddings in bowls for 5 minutes. Carefully loosen puddings. Turn onto a plate lined with baking paper, then turn upright onto plates. (Alternatively, serve in the bowls.)

5 For the chocolate fudge sauce, place chocolate and cream in a microwave-safe bowl. Microwave, uncovered, for 2-3 minutes on High/100%, stirring every minute with a metal spoon until smooth.

6 Drizzle puddings with warm sauce and serve with cream if desired.

Soft-centred puddings are just divine. The sugary crust on these is sensational.

To check the capacity of your bowls, pour 3/4 cup of water into a bowl. The water should come right to the top.

When travelling around Portugal, my girlfriend and I had two aims — one was to eat Portuguese custard tarts every day and the other was to learn how to make them. We achieved the first goal; but the recipe and art of a true Portuguese tart is a well-kept secret. This is a really good version.

Cheat's Portuguese custard tarts with sparkling affogato

makes 24 tarts (makes 1 affogato)

1 batch sweet shortcrust pastry (see page 238) or
  4 sheets frozen ready-rolled shortcrust pastry, partially thawed
4 egg yolks
$2/3$ cup caster sugar
1 teaspoon vanilla bean paste
$1^{1/2}$ tablespoons cornflour
2 cups milk
$1/4$ cup white sugar
2 teaspoons ground cinnamon

Sparkling affogato
$1/4$ cup freshly brewed double strength espresso
1 scoop vanilla ice-cream
chilled sparkling mineral water

1 Grease a 12-hole, 2-tablespoon capacity flat-based patty pan. If using sweet shortcrust pastry, roll out between baking paper until 5mm-thick. Using an 8cm cutter, cut 24 rounds from pastry. Use 12 pastry rounds to line patty pan holes. Prick pastry with a fork. Freeze tart cases for 10 minutes or until firm.

2 Preheat oven to 210°C no fan/200°C fan-forced. Bake tart cases blind (see page 239) for 8 minutes or until light golden. Remove the paper and rice and bake a further 3 minutes or until golden.

3 Whisk egg yolks, sugar and vanilla bean paste in a bowl until well combined. Add the cornflour and stir to combine. Add milk, $1/4$ cup at a time, whisking constantly until smooth. Transfer mixture to a saucepan over medium heat. Cook, stirring constantly, for 10-12 minutes or until custard just comes to the boil.

4 Carefully fill each warm tart case with warm custard. Bake for 8-10 minutes or until pastry is golden. Cool for 10 minutes in tray then remove to a wire rack. Repeat with remaining pastry and custard. Combine sugar and cinnamon and sprinkle over warm tarts.

5 For one sparkling affogato, pour hot coffee into a heatproof glass. Add the ice-cream and serve with mineral water to the side. Top affogato with mineral water to serve.

Cheat's Portuguese custard tarts with sparkling affogato

Roasted fruit with stirred vanilla custard

Roasted fruit with stirred vanilla custard

serves 4

1 bunch rhubarb, trimmed, cut into 3cm lengths
375g strawberries, hulled, halved
2 tablespoons vanilla sugar (see page 240)

Stirred vanilla custard
1 vanilla bean, halved lengthways
200ml pouring cream
3/4 cup milk
4 egg yolks
2 tablespoons caster sugar
3/4 teaspoon cornflour

1 Preheat oven to 230°C no fan/220°C fan-forced. Lightly grease a
3-cup capacity baking dish. Combine rhubarb and strawberries in the
dish, sprinkle with vanilla sugar, stir to coat all the fruit. Roast
for 10 minutes or until fruit is just tender. Remove from the oven
and stand for 5 minutes to produce syrup.

2 For the stirred vanilla custard, scrape black seeds from the centre
of the vanilla bean halves. Place cream, milk, vanilla bean halves
and seeds into a heavy-based saucepan over medium heat. Cook, stirring
often, for 10 minutes or until mixture just comes to the boil. Remove
vanilla beans, wash and set aside to dry.

3 Using an electric hand mixer, beat egg yolks, sugar and cornflour
until pale. Add the warm cream mixture and beat on low speed to
combine. Pour mixture back into saucepan and cook, stirring
constantly, over a low heat for 12 minutes or until custard thickens
and coats the wooden spoon (do not boil). Serve over roasted fruit.

There are a few good ready-made custards available in supermarkets, but you can't beat homemade — it's a knockout.

The dry vanilla bean can be used to make vanilla sugar (see page 240).

I learnt the art of pastry making from Lenotre, one of the world's best. This is the tart I baked in my exam. Yes, of course I got top marks! When you're passionate about something you usually excel.

Caramel walnut pear tart

serves 8

1 quantity sweet shortcrust pastry (see page 238) or
  2 sheets ready-rolled shortcrust pastry, partially thawed
1 cup white sugar
300ml thickened cream
50g butter, chopped
1 teaspoon vanilla extract
1 1/2 cups walnuts, roughly chopped
2 beurre bosc pears, peeled, quartered, cored
2 eggs, lightly beaten
cream or ice-cream, to serve

1 If using sweet shortcrust pastry, roll out between two sheets of baking paper to a 30cm round. Use the pastry to line base and sides of a 2.5cm-deep, 24cm (base) fluted loose-based flan pan. Freeze for 10 minutes or until firm.

2 Pour sugar into a clean, dry, non-stick frying pan over medium heat. Cook, stirring occasionally with a wooden spoon, until the sugar melts and turns deep golden. Remove from the heat, carefully pour in cream (sugar will crystalise). Return the pan to medium-high heat, cook stirring constantly for 8 minutes to dissolve the sugar. Simmer for 3 minutes until caramel thickens slightly. Remove from heat. Add the butter and vanilla and stir until smooth.

3 Preheat oven and a flat baking tray to 210°C no fan/200°C fan-forced. Prepare flan for baking blind (see page 239) then place on hot tray and bake for 8-10 minutes or until light golden around edges. Remove paper and rice. Bake for a further 8-10 minutes or until golden. Remove from oven. Reduce oven to 180°C no fan/170°C fan-forced.

4 Sprinkle walnuts over the warm pastry base. Thinly slice the pears and arrange over the walnuts. Stir eggs into cool caramel and pour it over the pears.

5 Bake tart for 20-25 minutes or until set in the centre. Set aside to cool to room temperature. Serve with cream or ice-cream.

Caramel walnut pear tart

Ginger, lime and bitters poached peaches

Ginger, lime and bitters poached peaches

serves 4

375ml bottle ginger beer
4 limes, juiced
2 cups white sugar
4 large or 8 small free-stone peaches or nectarines
1 tablespoon Angostura bitters
shortbread, to serve (see page 161)

Angostura bitters is available from liquor stores.

1 Combine ginger beer, $1/2$ cup lime juice and sugar in a large saucepan over low heat. Cook, stirring, for 3 minutes or until sugar has dissolved. Increase heat to high. Bring to the boil. Reduce heat to medium-low.

2 Cut a small cross in the base of each peach. Add peaches to the saucepan. Simmer gently, covered, for 5 minutes, or until peaches are just tender and skin begins to lift. Remove saucepan from heat. Using a slotted spoon, remove peaches from syrup.

3 Return syrup to the stove over high heat. Boil for 8-10 minutes or until syrup has reduced by half. Remove from the heat, stir in the bitters and set aside to cool.

4 Peel skin from peaches and discard. Place peaches in a bowl, pour the syrup over them and serve with shortbread.

Nan's bon vivant

serves 8

8 x 59g free-range eggs, separated
pinch cream of tartar
$1^1/3$ cups caster sugar
$2^1/2$ cups (250g) ground almonds (almond meal)
200g good-quality dark cooking chocolate
   (like Plaistowe or Club), chopped
250g butter, chopped
2 tablespoons cocoa powder

Kahlua cream
300ml double cream
2 tablespoons Kahlua liqueur

1 Preheat oven to 180°C no fan. Grease a 4.5cm-deep, 22.5cm x 28.5cm (base) slab pan. Line base and sides with baking paper allowing 2cm overhang at both long sides.

2 Using an electric mixer, beat egg whites and cream of tartar until soft peaks form. Using $2/3$ cup of the caster sugar, add 1 tablespoon at a time, beating after each addition until well combined. Fold the almonds through. Spread almond meringue over the base of prepared pan. Bake for 20 minutes or until light golden. Remove from oven. Reduce oven to 160°C no fan.

3 Combine chocolate and butter in a heatproof, microwave-safe bowl. Microwave, uncovered, for 2 minutes on High/100%, stirring every minute with a metal spoon until smooth. While warm, add the cocoa powder and stir to combine.

4 Using an electric mixer, beat egg yolks and remaining $2/3$ cup sugar until thick and pale. Add chocolate mixture and mix until well combined. Carefully pour the chocolate mixture over the almond meringue. Bake for 40 minutes or until a skewer inserted into centre comes out clean. Allow to cool completely in pan.

5 For the Kahlua cream, using a balloon whisk, whisk cream until stiff. Fold in Kahlua and refrigerate until ready to serve with bon vivant.

The bon vivant
will keep stored
in an airtight
container at room
temperature for
3-4 days.

Baked apples with crumble top

Baked apples with crumble top

serves 4

½ cup plain flour
1 teaspoon ground cinnamon
125g butter, chopped
½ cup firmly packed brown sugar
¼ cup rolled oats
4 golden delicious apples, halved, cored
vanilla custard (see page 185) or ice-cream, to serve

1 Preheat oven to 200°C no fan/180°C fan-forced. Lightly grease a baking dish.

2 Combine the flour and cinnamon in a large bowl. Add butter and use your fingertips to rub it into the flour until the mixture resembles coarse breadcrumbs. Stir in the brown sugar and oats, using fingers to mix until the crumble almost comes together.

3 Place the apples, cut side up, in the prepared dish. Press crumble mixture evenly over the apples. Bake for 15-20 minutes or until apples are just tender and the crumble is golden (if the top begins to brown too much, cover loosely with foil during cooking). Serve warm with vanilla custard or ice-cream.

This step can be done in a food processor if you have one.

This is a great mid-week dessert for the family at any time of year. The little crumbles are as good cold as they are hot. My mum used to make a big batch and give us leftovers in our lunchboxes.

Waffle french toast with espresso fruit

serves 4

1/2 cup pouring cream
2 tablespoons milk
3 eggs
2 tablespoons caster sugar
1/2 teaspoon vanilla extract
8 waffles
80g unsalted butter
thick cream, to serve (optional)

Espresso fruit
1/2 cup golden syrup
1/4 cup brown sugar
3/4 cup very strong brewed espresso coffee
375g dried fruit (pears, peaches, dates, figs, apples)

1 For the espresso fruit, combine golden syrup, brown sugar and coffee in a saucepan over medium heat. Cook 2-3 minutes, stirring until sugar has dissolved. Bring to the boil, boil uncovered for 10 minutes or until syrup has reduced by half. Add the dried fruit, cook 4-5 minutes or until fruit is soft and plump.

2 Meanwhile, combine cream, milk, eggs, sugar and vanilla in a shallow dish. Whisk with a fork until well combined.

3 Preheat oven to 190°C no fan/180°C fan-forced. Dip waffles one at a time in the cream mixture for 30 seconds each side or until well soaked. Hold over the dish to drain.

4 Heat 1 tablespoon of the butter in a large frying pan over medium heat until bubbling. Add two waffles, cook for 1-2 minutes each side or until golden. Transfer to a wire rack and keep warm on the rack in the oven. Repeat with remaining butter and waffles in three batches.

5 Place waffles onto plates, spoon fruit and syrup over. Serve with thick cream if desired.

Microwave apple and custard crumble

serves 6-8

This is a great 10-minute dessert. If you don't have a microwave, bake in the oven at 160°C fan-forced for 30 minutes.

800g can pie apples
2/3 cup thick purchased vanilla custard (Pauls brand)
1 packet butter cake mix (White Wings brand)
100g butter, chilled, thinly sliced
1/3 cup brown sugar
1/3 cup desiccated coconut, toasted
1/4 cup flaked almonds, toasted
1 teaspoon ground cinnamon
cream or ice-cream, to serve

1 Spoon pie apples into a 1.5-litre capacity heatproof, microwave-safe dish. Spoon custard over it. Sprinkle evenly with the dry butter cake mix. Place butter over the cake mix, covering it completely.

2 Combine sugar, coconut, almonds and cinnamon in a bowl and sprinkle over the butter.

3 Microwave, uncovered, for 8-10 minutes on Medium-high/70% or until the top is firm to touch and base is piping hot. Serve hot with cream or ice cream.

 To toast the coconut and almonds, place together in a non-stick frying pan and cook over medium-high heat, shaking pan often, until light golden.

Nan's cherry cream cheese strudel

serves 6

125g full-fat ricotta cheese
125g cream cheese, at room temperature, chopped
3 tablespoons caster sugar
1 teaspoon vanilla extract
1 egg
5 sheets filo pastry (Antonio brand)
80g clarified butter (ghee), melted
2 tablespoons packaged dry breadcrumbs
680g jar morello cherries, drained
1 tablespoon flaked almonds, toasted
pure icing sugar and vanilla ice-cream, to serve

1 If time allows, place ricotta into a nylon sieve over a bowl. Cover and refrigerate 1-2 hours to allow excess moisture to drain from the cheese.

2 Preheat oven to 200°C no fan. Line a large baking tray with baking paper. Using an electric mixer, beat ricotta, cream cheese, sugar and vanilla until smooth and creamy. Add egg and beat well.

3 Place one sheet of filo onto clean work surface. Brush with butter, top with a second sheet of filo, brush with butter and repeat the layering until you have five filo layers. Brush the top sheet well with butter.

4 Sprinkle breadcrumbs evenly over the filo. Spoon cream cheese mixture along one long edge. Top with cherries and sprinkle with almonds. Fold the ends in and roll up (not too tightly as the filling expands and the pastry may split) to secure filling. Place onto the prepared tray. Bake for 15 minutes, reduce the oven to 180°C no fan and bake a further 5-10 minutes until pastry is crisp and deep golden.

5 Allow to stand 15 minutes to cool a little. Dust heavily with icing sugar and serve.

Many of my nan's recipes were never translated. Luckily this one was. When I cooked it on Gourmet Safari on SBS television I was taken aback by the number of people who wanted the recipe. It's almost too good to share.

The strudel is long, so place diagonally on the baking tray.

Nan's cherry cream cheese strudel

Old-fashioned chocolate cake

Old-fashioned chocolate cake

serves 8

2 tablespoons cocoa powder
2 tablespoons boiling water
200g butter, softened
1 cup caster sugar
3 eggs, at room temperature
200g good-quality dark chocolate (like Plaistowe or Club), melted
1½ cups self-raising flour, sifted
⅓ cup milk

Filling
¾ cup thickened cream
125g mascarpone
2 tablespoons vanilla sugar (see page 240)

Chocolate icing
200g good-quality dark chocolate, chopped
½ cup thickened cream

1 Preheat oven to 170°C no fan. Grease and line the base and sides of three 20cm (base) sandwich pans with baking paper. Combine the cocoa powder and boiling water, stir until smooth.

2 Using an electric mixer, beat butter and sugar until pale and creamy. Add eggs, one at a time, beating well after each addition. Add melted chocolate and cocoa powder mixture and beat until well combined. Fold in half the flour until combined, then half the milk. Repeat with remaining flour and milk. Divide evenly among prepared pans and smooth the surface.

3 Bake cakes for 25-30 minutes or until a skewer inserted into the centre comes out clean. Stand cakes for 10 minutes in the pans before turning out onto a wire rack to cool completely.

4 For the filling, whip the cream until stiff peaks form, then fold in the mascarpone and sugar. Place one cake layer on a plate, spread with half the filling. Top with next cake layer, repeat with filling and final cake layer.

5 For the chocolate icing, combine chocolate and cream in a microwave-safe bowl. Microwave, uncovered, on High/100% in 1-minute bursts, stirring every minute with a metal spoon until smooth. Pour icing over the cake, allowing it to drizzle down the sides.

You can bake this cake in one 22cm (base) round cake pan for 40-45 minutes at 170°C no fan. Cut in half or in thirds with a serrated knife.

Don't add flour and milk at the same time — it will cause the flour to go lumpy.

Sugar-crusted crepes with mango

serves 4

12 frozen purchased crepes (Creative Gourmet brand), thawed
30g butter, melted
1/2 cup white sugar
2 mangoes, peeled, diced
2 tablespoons grated palm sugar
1/2 cup coconut cream, chilled

1 Warm the crepes following the packet directions, then carefully fold the crepes into quarters. Heat two large non-stick frying pans over high heat until hot. Brush the top of each folded crepe with butter then dip in white sugar to coat.

2 Place four crepes, sugar-side down into each pan and cook for 2-3 minutes or until sugar begins to melt. Carefully remove the crepes from the pan, re-dip in remaining white sugar and place back into hot frying pans. Cook 3-4 minutes or until sugar caramelises. Place hot crepes, sugar-side up on a plate.

3 Place mango and palm sugar in a bowl and toss gently to coat. Spoon into serving glasses or bowls, drizzle with a little coconut cream and serve with the hot crepes.

Fold the crepes while warm so they don't split.

This dessert is as easy as it looks. And believe me, you will find it hard to stop at three. Dessert-lovers will come back for more — guaranteed!

Sugar-crusted crepes with mango

Shaved pineapple with minted sugar

Shaved pineapple with minted sugar

serves 4

1 ripe pineapple
2 tablespoons mint leaves
1/2 cup demerara sugar
sorbet or ice-cream, to serve

1 Peel pineapple, removing all the eyes. Cut pineapple in half lengthways, then slice very thinly crossways.

2 Combine mint and sugar in a small food processor, process until almost crushed; alternatively combine in a bowl and crush with the end of a rolling pin.

3 Sprinkle the pineapple with minted sugar and stack on a plate. Serve with sorbet or ice-cream.

For the adult version of this recipe, a drizzle of chilled Malibu hits the spot.

Demerara sugar is a coarse golden sugar available in the baking aisle of supermarkets.

 Minted sugar can be stored in an airtight jar in the fridge for up to 2 weeks. It's delicious in iced tea.

Watermelon and lychees with passionfruit slush

Leftover
passionfruit
slush is delicious ....
spooned into
glasses and topped
up with chilled
gin or vodka
as a cocktail.

serves 4

1kg seedless watermelon
16 fresh lychees, peeled, seeds removed

Passionfruit slush
1 cup caster sugar
1 cup cold water
3 passionfruit, halved
4 limes, juiced

1 For the passionfruit slush, combine sugar and water in a medium saucepan over low heat. Cook, stirring, for 3 minutes or until sugar dissolves. Bring syrup to the boil, boil uncovered, without stirring, for 5 minutes or until syrup has reduced by half. Remove from the heat, stir in passionfruit pulp and $1/2$ cup lime juice. Pour into an airtight container and freeze for 2-3 hours or until semi-frozen.

2 Cut the watermelon into 2cm-thick slices, then cut each slice into 3-4cm triangles. Divide the watermelon and lychees among serving bowls, spoon the passionfruit slush over and serve.

 Fresh lychees are in season from November to February. Alternatively, you can use a 565g can, drained.

Watermelon and lychees with passionfruit slush

Clockwise from left: Strawberry and lime jam; Mango and vanilla bean jam; Peach and passionfruit jam variation (also on spoon); Brown sugar fig jam

Mango and vanilla bean jam

makes 2½ cups

Save the vanilla beans, wash and dry and use to make vanilla sugar (see page 240).

3 large mangoes, peeled
1¼ cups white sugar
1 large lemon, juiced
2 vanilla beans, split lengthways

1 Cut mango flesh from the stones and roughly chop. Place into a 3-litre capacity heatproof, microwave-safe bowl. Add the sugar and ⅓ cup lemon juice. Microwave, uncovered, for 4 minutes on High/100%. Stir to dissolve the sugar.

2 Scrape the seeds from vanilla beans. Add seeds and beans to the mango mixture. Microwave, uncovered, for a further 30–35 minutes on High/100%, stirring every 10 minutes, or until jam reaches setting point. Stand for 10 minutes.

3 Remove vanilla beans from jam. Spoon the hot jam into hot sterilised jars, then seal. Turn jars upside down for 2 minutes. Turn upright and allow to cool. Once opened, store in fridge for up to 3 months.

Variation
Peach and passionfruit jam Replace the mangoes with free-stone yellow peaches. Peel the peaches by cutting a cross in the base and standing them in a bowl of boiling water for 3 minutes. Stir the pulp of 2 large passionfruit into the jam at the end of step 2.

To test for setting point, place 1 teaspoon of jam onto a chilled saucer. Place saucer in freezer for 2 minutes or until jam cools to room temperature. Run your finger through the jam. If the surface wrinkles and the jam stays in two separate portions, it's ready to bottle. If not, cook for a little longer and retest.

Bought jam simply does not compare to homemade. Using the microwave is quick and easy and uses three-quarters less sugar than the conventional method. You may become like me and never purchase jam again.

Strawberry and lime jam

makes 1¹/4 cups

500g strawberries, washed, hulled, chopped
1 cup white sugar
2 limes or 1 large lemon, juiced

1 Place the strawberries into a 3-litre capacity heatproof microwave-safe bowl. Add the sugar and ¹/4 cup lime or lemon juice. Microwave, uncovered, for 4 minutes on High/100%. Stir to dissolve the sugar.

2 Microwave for a further 15 minutes on High/100% (jam should still be a little runny) or until jam reaches setting point (see page 207). Spoon the hot jam into hot sterilised jars and seal. Turn jars upside down for 2 minutes. Turn upright and allow to cool. Once opened, store in the fridge for up to 2 months.

Variation Replace the strawberries with fresh or frozen raspberries or blueberries or a mixture of all three berries. When using frozen berries the cooking time may be a little longer. Test using the method on page 207.

Brown sugar fig jam

makes 1^{1}/3 cups

500g fresh figs, chopped
1^{1}/2 cup brown sugar
2 large limes or lemons, juiced

1 Place the figs into a 3-litre capacity heatproof microwave-safe
bowl. Add the sugar and ^{1}/3 cup lime juice. Microwave, uncovered, for
4 minutes on High/100%. Stir to dissolve the sugar.

2 Microwave for a further 15 minutes on High/100% (jam should still
be a little runny) or until jam reaches setting point (see page 207).
Spoon the hot jam into hot sterilised jars and seal. Turn jars upside
down for 2 minutes. Turn upright and allow to cool. Once opened, store
in the fridge for up to 2 months.

Variation You can replace the fresh figs with fresh or canned plums.

When figs are in season cook a few batches of this jam. While
it's great on toast and scones, a large dollop on sugar-crusted
crepes (see page 200) is simply irresistible.

Our Christmas and summer holidays are huge family affairs where plenty of food and drink is consumed. These cocktails are always in the freezer, ready to scoop and drink. They keep for up to 6 months.

Frozen cosmopolitan

serves 10

500ml classic cranberry juice
500ml vodka
6 large limes, juiced, strained

Sugar syrup
2 cups white sugar
2 cups cold water

1 For the sugar syrup, combine the sugar and water in a large saucepan over medium heat. Cook, stirring occasionally, for 5 minutes or until sugar has dissolved. Increase heat to medium-high, bring syrup to the boil without stirring, boil gently for 10 minutes or until syrup thickens slightly. Remove from the heat. Set aside to cool.

2 Pour sugar syrup into a 3-litre container. Stir in cranberry juice, vodka and 1 cup of lime juice. Cover and freeze overnight.

3 Stir frozen cosmopolitan and scoop into glasses. Serve immediately.

Frozen cosmopolitan

Frozen mango daiquiri

serves 10

2 cups mango puree
500ml Bacardi rum
4 large limes, juiced, strained

Sugar syrup
2 cups white sugar
2 cups cold water

1 For the sugar syrup, combine the sugar and water in a large saucepan over medium heat. Cook, stirring occasionally, for 5 minutes or until sugar has dissolved. Increase heat to medium-high, bring syrup to the boil without stirring, boil gently for 10 minutes or until syrup thickens slightly. Remove from the heat. Set aside to cool.

2 Pour the sugar syrup into a 3-litre container. Stir in mango puree, rum and 2/3 of a cup lime juice. Cover and freeze overnight.

3 Stir frozen mango daiquiri and scoop into glasses. Serve immediately.

 Four large mangoes or two 300g packets of frozen mango, thawed, will give you 2 cups of puree. You can replace the mango with berries, lychees or passionfruit pulp.

Watermelon mai tai

serves 10

800g seedless watermelon, peeled, chopped, chilled
2/3 cup pineapple juice
2/3 cup white rum
1/3 cup triple sec liqueur
2 teaspoons grenadine
crushed ice, to serve

1 Combine half the watermelon, half the pineapple juice, half the rum, half the triple sec liqueur and half the grenadine in a blender and blend until smooth. Pour into a chilled jug. Repeat with remaining ingredients.

2 Spoon ice into base of each glass until one-third full. Pour in watermelon mixture and serve.

Pineapple and coconut mocktail

serves 10

2 sweet ripe pineapples, peeled, cored, roughly chopped
4 cups ice cubes
2 tablespoons maple syrup
400ml can coconut milk (Ayam brand), chilled

1 Combine half the pineapple, half the ice cubes, half the maple syrup and half the coconut milk in a blender and blend until smooth. Pour into a chilled jug. Repeat with remaining ingredients.

2 Pour into chilled glasses and serve.

A non-alcoholic version of this is just as good (well, almost) and it's important for the kids and designated drivers not to feel left out. Replace the rum, triple sec and grenadine with 1 cup of chilled sugar syrup (see page 210) and use unsweetened pineapple juice.

Fabulous inspirations

Raspberry and Malteser ice-cream

Crush Maltesers and semi-frozen raspberries then fold into softened vanilla ice-cream. Re-freeze ice-cream mixture. Serve scoops in cones or in a parfait glass, drizzled with warm chocolate fudge sauce (see page 181).

Lemon cream biscuits with sorbet

Use a serrated knife to split large sponge finger biscuits in half. Swirl mascarpone and lemon curd (see page 153) together and sandwich between biscuit halves. Cover and let stand for 15 minutes to soften slightly. Serve with lemon sorbet.

Baked meringue trifle

Spoon fresh or thawed frozen berries into heatproof glasses. Pour over bought custard. Top with cubes of sponge or Madeira cake soaked in a little liqueur (for adults) or fruit juice (for kids). Top with a spoonful of meringue (see page 153) and bake until golden.

Jam roll ice-cream cake

Layer slices of jam roll over the base of a springform cake
pan. Top with a thick layer of softened vanilla ice-cream.
Press more slices of jam roll over the ice-cream and freeze
until firm. Cut into wedges and serve.

Honeycomb figs

Cut a cross in the top of fresh figs. Beat fresh ricotta with
finely chopped Violet Crumble bar and spoon into the centre
of the figs. Drizzle with honey and serve cold, or warm in
190°C no fan/180°C fan-forced oven for 5 minutes.

Melon frappé

Blend or process chopped chilled rockmelon with vanilla ice-cream
and ice cubes until thick and slushie-like. Spoon into glasses
and serve with shortbread (see page 161).

Caramel baked pineapple

Trim the top and base of a small pineapple. Cut pineapple into quarters lengthways, then score at 1cm intervals. Place on a baking tray. Combine a little melted butter, brown sugar and vanilla and spoon over the pineapple. Roast in a hot oven until golden and warmed through. Serve with sorbet.

Toffee mangoes

Cut the cheeks off fresh mangoes. Brush with Marsala or Kahlua and dip in brown sugar. Heat a frying pan over high heat until hot, then place a sheet of baking paper into the hot pan. Press the mango cheeks, sugar-side down, onto the paper and cook until caramelised. Serve with coconut ice-cream.

Chocolate berry brioche

Spread toasted brioche thickly with Nutella then top with slices of fresh strawberries. Grill until strawberries are warm. Serve with a scoop of ice-cream.

Chocolate caramel tarts

Warm buttersnap cookies in the oven for a few minutes until soft,
press into a patty pan and allow to cool, forming a little
case. Whisk a can of bought caramel until smooth and spoon
into the cases. Pour melted chocolate over and allow to set.
Alternatively, fill with sweetened mascarpone and strawberries.

Ricotta fritters

Beat fresh ricotta with an egg yolk and enough self-raising flour
to form a thick mixture. Sweeten with vanilla sugar (see page 240).
Drop spoonfuls of mixture into hot oil and deep-fry until golden.
Drizzle with honey and sprinkle with chopped pistachio nuts.
Serve hot with cream or custard.

Chocolate berry tiramisu cups

Dip sponge finger biscuits into strong brewed coffee. Break and
arrange over the base of serving glasses. Combine equal amounts
mascarpone and whipped cream and sweeten with sugar and vanilla.
Spoon mixture over the biscuits, top with a spoonful of bought
chocolate custard and a handful of berries. Repeat the layers.
Refrigerate for 1-2 hours before serving.

Essentials

The basics are often overlooked in cookbooks and magazines, which is why I wanted to include as many as I could here. I hope you find what follows to be useful. It's valuable information I have been gathering since I first started cooking.

Scrambled eggs

serves 2

4 free-range eggs, at room temperature
1/4 cup pouring cream or milk
25g butter, chopped
toast, croissants or bagels, to serve

1 Whisk the eggs and cream or milk together for 2 minutes. The egg should fall in a thin stream from the whisk. Stand for a couple of minutes to let the foam settle.

2 Heat a medium 20cm (base) non-stick frying pan over medium heat until hot. Add the butter to hot frying pan and swirl quickly to coat the base. As the very last of the butter melts, pour in the egg mixture. Cook for 1 minute or until the eggs start to set.

3 Using a spatula or flat-edged wooden spoon, push the set egg mixture toward the centre of pan, tilting the pan to allow the uncooked mixture to run over the base. Cook for a further 40-50 seconds or until the egg mixture forms creamy curds, but is not completely cooked. Remove the pan from the heat, as the eggs will continue to cook. Spoon the eggs onto toast, croissants or bagels and season with salt and pepper. Serve.

Don't add salt at this stage. It will cause the eggs to toughen and weep during cooking.

Boiled eggs

serves 4

½ teaspoon salt flakes
4 free-range eggs, at room temperature

1 Half-fill a saucepan with cold water. Add the salt and bring to a gentle boil over high heat (the saucepan should be just large enough to contain the eggs in a single layer).

2 Place one egg at a time onto a large metal spoon and lower into the water. When all the eggs are in the water, stir gently for 30 seconds (this helps to centre the yolks).

3 Reduce the heat to medium: it should be gently simmering. For soft boiled (a runny yolk and well-set white) cook for 4 minutes; for medium boiled egg (semi-firm yolk and firm white) cook for 5 minutes; for hard boiled, cook for 8 minutes.

4 Remove the eggs with a slotted spoon. Rinse under cold water to stop the cooking process. Tap the shell a few times and allow to cool completely before peeling.

The shell will peel easier from slightly older eggs than from farm-fresh ones.

Tomato passata sauce

makes 2¹/₂ cups

2 tablespoons olive oil
1 brown onion, finely chopped
2 large garlic cloves, crushed
800g can whole peeled tomatoes
pinch of white sugar
1¹/₂ teaspoons dried oregano

1 Heat oil in a saucepan over medium heat. Add onion and garlic and cook for 5 minutes or until onion is soft. Add tomatoes, sugar and a good pinch of salt and pepper. Cook, breaking up the tomatoes with a wooden spoon, for 10 minutes or until sauce comes to the boil.

2 Reduce heat to medium-low, simmer for 10 minutes for pasta sauce or 15 minutes for pizza sauce. Allow to cool slightly. Place in food processor and process until smooth. Stir in oregano, taste and adjust the seasonings. Tomato passata sauce will keep in a sterilised jar in the fridge for up to 2 months.

Beautiful Bolognese sauce

makes 6 cups

2 tablespoons olive oil
1 large brown onion, finely chopped
2 rashers bacon, rind removed, finely chopped
2 garlic cloves, crushed
1/3 cup tomato paste
375g veal mince
375g beef mince
1/2 cup dry white wine or chicken stock
800g whole peeled tomatoes, roughly chopped
2 teaspoons caster sugar
2 fresh or 1 dried bay leaf
1/2 cup semi-dried tomatoes, finely chopped

1 Heat oil in a large heavy-based saucepan over medium heat. Add onion, bacon and garlic. Cook, stirring often, for 5 minutes or until onion is soft. Add tomato paste and cook, stirring, for 1 minute. Increase heat to high.

2 Add mince, cook, breaking up mince with a wooden spoon, for 5 minutes or until browned. Add wine or stock and bring to the boil. Stir in tomatoes, sugar, bay leaves and semi-dried tomatoes. Bring to the boil, reduce heat to medium-low and simmer, uncovered, for 1 hour or until thick. Remove the bay leaves. Season with salt and pepper.

If I have time, instead of simmering the Bolognese on the stove for 1 hour, I cook it for 4 hours in the oven at 130°C no fan — covered for the first 2 hours, then uncovered for the final 2 hours. The colour, flavour and aroma are even more sensational.

This pizza dough does not need to prove, but it is important to make sure you knead it enough (5–8 minutes) to develop the gluten.

Quick mix pizza dough

makes 2 pizzas

3/4 cup warm water
7g sachet instant dried yeast
pinch of salt
1/2 teaspoon caster sugar
2 tablespoons olive oil
2 cups plain flour
80g parmesan cheese, finely grated

1 Combine water, yeast, salt, sugar and oil in a jug, stir to combine. Sift flour into a large bowl, stir in parmesan. Add yeast mixture and mix to form a soft dough.

2 Turn dough onto a lightly floured surface and knead for 8 minutes or until elastic. When you press the top of the dough it should bounce back and leave no indentation.

3 Cut the dough in half and roll each piece out to a 22cm x 34cm rectangle. For thin crust, top immediately as desired (see page 23). For a thick crust, allow the dough to stand at room temperature for 10-15 minutes before topping. Bake 15-20 minutes at 220°C fan-forced.

Couscous

serves 4

1½ cups couscous
1½ cups boiling water or stock
1 tablespoon extra virgin olive oil

1 Pour the couscous into a heatproof bowl. Pour over the boiling water or stock, stir to coat the grains. Cover tightly and stand for 3 minutes or until water or stock is absorbed.

2 Remove the cover, drizzle with olive oil, stir gently with a fork to separate grains. Season with salt and pepper and serve.

Mashed potato

serves 4

1kg sebago, pontiac, king edward, or
   lady christl potatoes, unpeeled
60g butter, chopped
200ml hot milk or cream

1 Place the whole potatoes in a large saucepan, cover with cold water. Cover and bring to the boil over high heat. Remove the lid, reduce heat to medium-high. Boil, uncovered, for 30 minutes or until the potatoes are tender when tested with a skewer.

2 Use a slotted spoon to transfer the potatoes to a colander. Set aside for 5 minutes or until cool enough to handle. Use a small sharp knife to peel and discard the skins.

3 Drain the water from the pan and return the potatoes to the dry hot saucepan. Shake the saucepan over low heat for 1-2 minutes to remove any remaining moisture from the potatoes.

4 Use a potato masher to mash the potatoes. Add the butter and milk or cream and stir with a wooden spoon until smooth. Season with salt and pepper. Serve.

Shortcut Replace steps 1 & 2 above with the following if you are in a hurry. Peel potatoes and cut into large chunks. Cook in a large saucepan of boiling salted water for 20 minutes or until very tender but not falling apart.

Pour the milk or cream into a microwave-safe jug or cup. Microwave, uncovered, for 1-2 minutes on High/100% or until hot.

Squashed potatoes

serves 6

1.2kg (about 24) chat potatoes
olive oil cooking spray

1 Preheat oven to 250°C no fan/250°C fan-forced. Place the potatoes in a large saucepan, cover with cold water, and bring to the boil. Reduce heat to medium and simmer, uncovered, for 15-20 minutes or until just tender. Drain.

2 Lightly grease a large roasting pan or tray. Tip the hot potatoes into the roasting pan and flatten each potato using the heel of your hand or a potato masher.

3 Spray the potatoes with olive oil and season with salt and pepper. Roast for 15-20 minutes or until golden and crisp.

The oven temperature is the same with or without the fan. If you use the fan, it will take 15 minutes to crispen.

The best roast potatoes

serves 4

1kg sebago, coliban, king edward or golden delight potatoes,
  peeled, cut into 6cm pieces
olive oil

1 Preheat oven to 220°C no fan/200°C fan-forced. Place the potatoes in a large saucepan. Cover with cold water. Bring to the boil, covered, over high heat. Reduce heat to medium. Partially cover saucepan and simmer for 15 minutes or until potatoes are just tender when pierced with a knife.

2 Drain potatoes well. Return to the hot saucepan over low heat. Cook, gently shaking saucepan, for 2 minutes or until any remaining water evaporates. Turn off the heat. Cover saucepan and shake vigorously to roughen surface of potatoes (this will make them crunchy when roasted).

3 Pour enough oil into a large roasting pan to cover the base with a thin layer. Place in oven for 5 minutes or until hot. Working quickly, add potatoes to hot oil. Turn to coat. Return to the oven. Roast for 30 minutes or until base is golden. Turn potatoes. Cook for a further 25-30 minutes or until crisp and golden. Season with salt. Serve.

Twice-fried chips

serves 4

1kg sebago, spunta, king edward or bintje potatoes, peeled
peanut oil, for deep-frying

Peanut oil will get hotter than other oils, giving you crisp, crunchy golden chips.

1 Cut the potatoes into long chips about 1.5cm-thick. Pat dry with paper towels.

2 Fill a large saucepan, wok or deep-fryer with peanut oil until half-full. Heat over medium heat until a small piece of potato skin sizzles when dropped into the oil (it should not be too hot at this stage, as you are only blanching the chips).

3 Preheat oven to 190°C no fan/180°C fan-forced.

4 Place a wire rack over a large oven tray lined with paper towels. Divide chips into three batches. Deep-fry chips, one batch at a time, for 5 minutes or until they just start to colour around the edges. Use a slotted spoon to transfer chips to the wire rack. Repeat with remaining two batches, allowing the oil to reheat between batches. When all the chips have been blanched, allow to cool for 10 minutes.

5 Reheat the oil over medium-high heat until hot. Deep-fry the chips again, in batches, for 8-10 minutes or until crisp and golden. Keep the cooked chips warm on the rack in oven while cooking remaining chips. Season with salt. Serve immediately.

To make shoestring chips, cut the potatoes into long 5mm-thin chips.

Prepackaged stock
is convenient but
expensive and
has nowhere near
the flavour of
homemade. Here
are two versions
— the overnight
one and the quick
microwave type.
Both are fantastic.

Homemade chicken stock

makes 2 litres

1.5kg chicken wings, rinsed
2.5-3 litres cold water
1 brown onion, unpeeled, sliced
1 large carrot, unpeeled, cut into 5cm pieces
1 stalk celery (with leaves), roughly chopped
2 bay leaves
1 sprig thyme
2 sprigs flat-leaf parsley
6 peppercorns

1 Place chicken wings into a large stock pot. Add the water and bring to the boil, uncovered, over medium heat. Every 10 minutes, use a slotted spoon to skim the surface of the stock.

2 Once the water has come to the boil, add the carrot and celery. Tie the remaining ingredients in a piece of muslin and add to the pot. Simmer gently (small bubbles should break the surface) for 3 hours. Set aside for 2 hours to cool.

3 Strain the stock (do not press through sieve) into a large bowl, cover and refrigerate overnight. Remove the fat set on the surface of the stock. Freeze or use as desired.

Shortcut Combine 500g chicken wings and 1 roughly chopped unpeeled brown onion, 1 carrot and 1 stalk celery in a 3-litre heatproof microwave-safe bowl. Add 2 bay leaves, sprig thyme, sprig parsley and 6 peppercorns. Cover with cold water. Cover with two layers of plastic wrap and microwave for 10 minutes on High/100%. Remove plastic wrap and microwave for 30 minutes on Medium/50%. Strain and use as desired.

To freeze, line a jug with a snap lock bag, pour 2 cups stock into the bag then place in the freezer until firm. Secure the bag and freeze.

Fried rice

serves 6 as side

2 cups long-grain rice, rinsed
1¹/₂ tablespoons peanut oil
2 eggs, lightly beaten
1 brown onion, halved, thinly sliced
4 rashers bacon, rind removed, chopped
300g green prawns, peeled, deveined, roughly chopped
4 green onions, thinly sliced
1 small red capsicum, diced
¹/₄ small Chinese cabbage, finely shredded
¹/₂ cup frozen peas
2 tablespoons kecap manis (ABC brand)
1 tablespoon soy sauce
1 red chilli, thinly sliced, to serve (optional)
¹/₄ cup fried shallots, to serve (optional)

1 Cook rice following absorption method on the packet or microwave method (see page 232). Spread onto a baking tray. Cool to room temperature, cover and refrigerate for 2 hours or until cold.

2 Heat a wok over medium heat until hot. Add 2 teaspoons oil and swirl to coat the wok. Add egg and swirl to form a wafer-thin omelette. Cook for 30 seconds or until egg sets. Slide onto a board, roll omelette, then thinly slice crossways.

3 Wipe the wok clean and heat over high heat until hot. Add remaining oil and swirl to coat the wok. Add the onion and bacon, and stir-fry for 2 minutes or until onion is soft. Add the prawns and stir-fry for 1-2 minutes or until prawns turn pink.

4 Add the rice, green onions, capsicum, cabbage, peas and combined kecap manis and soy sauce. Stir-fry for 4 minutes or until rice is heated through. Add the sliced omelette and stir to combine. Sprinkle with chopped chilli and fried shallots if desired. Serve.

 Fried shallots are inexpensive from Asian grocery stores, and they add a lovely crunch to the finished dish. Once opened, store in the freezer to prevent them from becoming rancid.

Long-grain rice is best cooked and chilled the day before making the fried rice.

This method is foolproof. I wish I could take credit for it but my baby sister Wendy showed me how to do it! The beauty of food and cooking is you're always learning.

Microwave steamed rice

serves 4

1¹/₃ cups white basmati, long grain or jasmine rice

1 Place rice in a sieve and rinse under cold water until the water runs clear (this removes excess starch and prevents the rice turning gluggy). Tip the rice into a microwave rice-cooker or 2-litre plastic or Pyrex bowl.

2 Pour in enough cold water so it sits 2.5-3cm above the level of the rice (easy way to judge this is to place your index finger on top of the rice; the water should reach the first line/joint on your finger). Cover with the lid or a double layer of plastic wrap.

3 Place a sheet of baking paper onto microwave turntable (this helps catch spills if there are any). Microwave for 5 minutes on High/100% then 7 minutes on Medium/50% for any quantity. Allow to stand, covered, for 5 minutes. Carefully remove the lid, stir gently with a fork and serve.

Microwave chilli jam

makes 1 1/2 cups

6 red birds eye chillies, roughly chopped
4 large red banana chillies, roughly chopped
1 small red onion, peeled, chopped
3 large garlic cloves, crushed
1/2 cup cold water
1 teaspoon salt flakes
2 cups white sugar
1/2 cup red wine vinegar
1/3 cup port

1 Place chillies (including seeds and membranes), onion, garlic, water and salt into a food processor and process until finely chopped. Transfer mixture to a 12-cup capacity, heatproof, microwave-safe bowl. Stir in sugar, vinegar and port.

2 Microwave chilli mixture, uncovered, for 3 minutes on High/100%, stirring every minute, or until sugar has dissolved.

3 Microwave, uncovered, for a further 20-25 minutes on High/100% or until jam reaches setting point. Spoon the hot jam into hot sterilised jars and seal. Turn jars upside down for 2 minutes. Turn upright and allow to cool. Once opened, store in the fridge for up to 12 weeks. Use in casseroles, stir-fries and Asian soups or on sandwiches and pizzas.

To test for setting point, place 1 teaspoon of jam onto a chilled saucer. Place saucer in freezer for 2 minutes or until jam cools to room temperature. Run your finger through the jam. If the surface wrinkles and the jam stays in two separate portions, it's ready to bottle. If not, cook for a little longer and retest.

Roasted capsicum

Red and yellow capsicums are the best ones to use.

2 red capsicum
2 yellow capsicum

1 Cut the capsicums into quarters, remove the centre core and all the seeds.

2 Preheat a grill on high. Place the capsicum skin-side up onto a baking tray (don't line with baking paper as it will burn). Grill for 6-8 minutes or until the skin turns black. Transfer capsicum into a snap lock bag and seal. Stand for 5 minutes (the steam helps to lift the skin).

3 Use your fingers to peel and remove the skin (avoid rinsing under cold water as this dilutes the flavour). Cut capsicum into strips and use on sandwiches, pizzas, burgers or in salads, casseroles or Bolognese. Alternatively, place into a clean sterilised jar, cover with olive oil, seal and store in the fridge for up to 2 months.

Char-grilled vegetables

1 bunch rosemary
$\frac{1}{4}$ cup olive oil
1 red capsicum, quartered, cored and seeds removed
1 yellow capsicum, quartered, cored and seeds removed
1 eggplant, cut into 1cm-thick rounds or lengths
2 zucchini, cut into 1cm-thick lengths
12 button mushrooms, trimmed
1 sweet potato, peeled, cut into 5mm-thick rounds
$\frac{1}{2}$ butternut pumpkin, cut into 5mm-thick slices

1 Preheat a char-grill plate or barbecue grill over high until very hot. Using a small bunch of rosemary as a brush (pastry brush bristles will burn), lightly grease the plate.

2 Brush both sides of the vegetables with olive oil. Reduce heat to medium-high and cook vegetables for 3-4 minutes each side or until tender and slightly charred. Set aside to cool. Cut the capsicum into strips.

3 Use immediately or store in an airtight container drizzled with olive oil in the fridge for up to 10 days.

This is about
1 large bunch.

Basil pesto

makes 1¹/4 cups

2 cups firmly packed fresh basil leaves
¹/4 cup pine nuts, toasted
3 garlic cloves, roughly chopped
²/3 cup extra virgin olive oil
100g freshly grated parmesan cheese (optional)
extra virgin olive oil, for covering

1 Place the basil, pine nuts and garlic in a small food processor. Process, stopping processor and scraping down sides occasionally, until evenly chopped.

2 With processor running, pour the oil through the spout in a slow and steady stream until all the oil has been incorporated. Transfer pesto to a bowl. Stir in the parmesan (if using) and season with salt and pepper. Use immediately, or prepare for storing.

3 Use pesto immediately or, to store, transfer pesto to a clean, sterilised jar. Cover the surface of the pesto with a thin layer of extra virgin olive oil (this prevents it from discolouring and growing mould). Store in the fridge for up to 3 months. Each time you use some, remember to recover the surface with oil.

Vinaigrette

makes $1/3$ cup

$1/4$ cup extra virgin olive oil
1 tablespoon red wine vinegar
1 teaspoon caster sugar
1 teaspoon Dijon mustard
$1/2$ small clove garlic, crushed

1 Place all the ingredients in a screw-top jar and season with sea salt and freshly ground black pepper. Shake the jar well to combine.

2 Pour dressing over salad just before serving.

 I don't remember the last time I bought dressing. You can replace the red wine vinegar with balsamic, herb-flavoured or cider vinegar. The vinegar can also be replaced with 2 tablespoons fresh lemon, lime or orange juice.

Shortcrust pastry

enough for 26cm (base) tart pan

1¹/₂ cups plain flour
125g butter, chilled, cubed
1 egg, whisked
2-3 tablespoons chilled water

1 Place the flour and butter in a food processor and process until mixture resembles breadcrumbs. Add the egg and 2 tablespoons water. Process until pastry just comes together in a ball, adding remaining water if necessary.

2 Turn pastry onto a lightly floured surface and knead gently until smooth. Press into a 15cm round then wrap in greaseproof paper (don't use plastic as this causes pastry to sweat). Refrigerate for 15 minutes or until firm enough to roll out.

Variation For sweet shortcrust pastry, add ¹/₃ cup pure icing sugar with the flour in step 1 and use 2 egg yolks instead of 1 egg.

Rolling out homemade pastry

1 Place chilled pastry disc between two large sheets of baking paper. Use a rolling pin to roll the pastry, turning a quarter turn after each roll (this helps keep the pastry in an even shape). Roll out 6cm larger than the base of the tart pan to allow for the side of the pan. Remove the top sheet of baking paper. Feel the pastry. If it's still nice and firm and cool to touch, sprinkle a little flour over the surface and roll over the rolling pin; if not, refrigerate for 10 minutes until it is.

2 Unroll the pastry over the tart pan. Lift the edges and ease into the pan. Using scissors, trim the excess pastry so it sits just above the top of the pan (this allows for a little shrinkage). Refrigerate or freeze until firm.

Baking blind

1 Pierce the base of the uncooked pastry with a fork six times (this helps prevent the pastry from bubbling up during cooking). Scrunch up and then flatten out a piece of greaseproof baking paper 6cm larger than the base of the pastry case (the rough surface of paper from scrunching stops the pastry sticking to the paper). Use the paper to line the base and side of the pastry case. Half fill the pastry case with baking beans, dried rice or raw dried pasta (this prevents the pastry rising and helps to keep the shape of pastry).

2 Bake as per the recipe. Remove the beans and paper (the pastry should be set and light golden at this stage). Return to the oven, and continue following the recipe. Always allow the beans, rice or pasta to cool completely before storing for re-use.

Baking blind prevents the pastry from becoming soggy on the base when the filling is added.

When cooking with vanilla beans, a recipe will often require you to scrape out the seeds and sometimes immerse the bean in warm milk, cream or syrup to extract flavour. Don't throw the bean away. After use, strain then rinse the bean in cold water and leave it on a wire rack overnight. Place the dry bean into the jar of caster sugar.

Vanilla sugar

makes 1 cup

1 vanilla bean
1 cup caster sugar

1 To start your jar of sugar, split the bean in half with a sharp knife, leaving the black seeds in the pod. Place the split vanilla bean into an airtight jar. Pour the sugar over the top. Secure the lid and shake to coat. Leave to stand for one month.

2 Keep topping up the sugar as you use it and adding dry used vanilla beans to maintain the intensity.

Harissa

makes 3/4 cup

2 red capsicums, halved, roasted, skin removed
12 red birds eye chillies, halved
2 large garlic cloves, crushed
2 teaspoons ground cumin
1 teaspoon ground coriander
1 teaspoon salt flakes
2 tablespoons extra virgin olive oil

1 Use a small teaspoon to remove the seeds and membrane from the capsicums.

2 Place all ingredients in a small food processor and process until smooth; alternatively, pound in a mortar with the pestle.

3 Spoon mixture into a sterilised jar, cover the top with a thin layer of olive oil and refrigerate for up to 6 months.

Harissa is a very hot chilli paste. To reduce the heat, remove the seeds and membrane from half the chillies.

This can be used as an oil-free salad dressing or dipping sauce (see page 70). I make it and keep in the fridge for up to 2 months. The longer you keep it, the spicier it becomes.

Nuoc cham

makes 5 cups

8 garlic cloves, chopped
4 red banana chillies, roughly chopped
1 small red chilli, seeds removed, roughly chopped
2/3 cup caster sugar
4 large limes, juiced
1 cup fish sauce
2 cups cold water

1 Place the garlic, banana chilli (including the seeds), red chilli, sugar and 3/4 cup of lime juice in a blender or food processor. Blend or process until well combined. Pour into a jug. Stir in the fish sauce and cold water.

2 Pour the sauce into a clean airtight jar and place in the fridge for 24 hours, shaking occasionally, to allow the flavours to develop.

Bechamel sauce

makes 5 cups

60g butter, chopped
1/2 cup plain flour
5 cups milk
1/4 teaspoons sea salt
pinch ground nutmeg

Freshly ground nutmeg has a much better flavour than pre-ground nutmeg.

1 Melt the butter in a medium saucepan over medium-high heat until foaming. Add the flour all at once. Cook, stirring, for 1-2 minutes or until bubbling. Remove the pan from the heat. Slowly add the milk, whisking constantly, until sauce is smooth.

2 Return the pan to the heat and cook, stirring with a wooden spoon, for 10 minutes or until sauce comes to the boil. Remove the pan from the heat. Stir in the nutmeg and season with salt and pepper. Cover the surface of the sauce with plastic wrap to prevent a skin forming.

 Bechamel sauce can be made ahead, but it will thicken on standing. Don't thin it down, just beat really well before reheating.

Essential vegie inspirations

I am asked daily about new ways to serve vegetables so they don't fade into the background. Here are some simple ways to add variety to mid-week vegies.

Balsamic bean bundles

Steam, microwave or blanch green beans. Wrap a slice of prosciutto around 6 beans to form bundles. Pan-fry the bean bundles in a non-stick frying pan in a little olive oil until prosciutto is crisp. Drizzle with honey and balsamic dressing (see page 110).

Basil pesto beans

Steam, microwave or blanch green beans. Add a large spoonful of basil pesto (see page 236) and finely grated parmesan cheese, toss to coat. Serve warm or cold.

Mustard corn

Steam, microwave or blanch fresh or frozen corn cobs. Whisk olive oil, a teaspoon Dijon mustard and a drizzle of maple syrup together, drizzle over the corn and turn to coat.

Lemon-scented broccoli

Finely grate the rind of 1 large lemon into a screw-top jar, add extra virgin olive oil, salt and pepper and shake well. Steam, microwave or blanch broccoli florets until bright green, then drain well. Drizzle with lemon oil and toss to coat.

Beans with garlic hazelnut crumbs

Pan-fry a handful of coarse sourdough breadcrumbs in a little
crushed garlic and olive oil until light golden. Add roughly
chopped hazelnuts and grated lemon rind. Sprinkle over steamed,
microwaved or blanched green beans.

Spiced buttered corn

Blend a large spoonful softened butter with a sprinkling of
ground cumin, coriander, garam masala, chilli powder and salt
flakes. Dollop over steamed, microwaved or blanched corn cobs.

Wok-tossed broccoli

Sauté finely chopped garlic, ginger, lemongrass and green chilli
in a little peanut oil until aromatic. Add broccoli florets and
stir-fry until just tender.

Wasabi corn

Blend softened butter with wasabi paste to taste, season with
salt and spoon over steamed, microwaved or blanched corn cobs.

Shaved broccoli with bacon and walnuts

Sauté finely chopped bacon in a little olive oil until light golden. Add a handful chopped walnuts and cook until toasted. Add washed and thinly sliced broccoli to the hot pan. Drizzle with a little olive oil and toss over high heat until broccoli turns bright green. Season with salt and pepper.

Parmesan carrots

Peel and cut carrots in quarters lengthways. Combine equal quantities dry breadcrumbs and grated parmesan cheese on a plate. Dip carrots in flour, egg and then the breadcrumb mixture, pressing to secure. Drizzle with a little olive oil and roast in hot oven until golden and tender.

Orange mustard carrots

Heat 2 tablespoons each olive oil, orange juice and brown sugar in a frying pan over high heat. Add a dollop of seeded mustard and peeled, chopped carrots. Toss over medium-high heat until dressing reduces and carrots are just tender. Season.

Peas with nuoc cham dressing

Steam, microwave or blanch peas until just tender, drain well. Drizzle with nuoc cham (see page 242) and toss to coat.

Maple coconut carrots

Peel and cut carrots into matchsticks. Steam, microwave or blanch carrots. Meanwhile, toast a handful shredded or flaked coconut in a frying pan until light golden. Add the well-drained carrots and a drizzle of maple syrup or honey. Add a drizzle of olive oil and toss until well coated.

Creamy roasted peas

Steam, microwave or blanch peas until they turn bright green, then drain well and tip into a baking dish. Crumble over creamy feta cheese, goats cheese or ricotta cheese. Sprinkle with just a few fresh breadcrumbs and drizzle with olive oil. Roast 5-10 minutes or until top is light golden.

Peas with ginger marmalade and almonds

Warm a large dollop of ginger marmalade in a frying pan over medium heat. Add steamed, microwaved or blanched peas and sauté until well coated. Sprinkle toasted almonds over and a few dried currants (if you have them), and toss to coat.

Things I love

Cake pans

My wish list for every kitchen: 2 large flat baking trays; 24cm loose-bottom tart pan; 20 and 23cm springform cake pans; 20cm (base) round cake pan; 20cm square (base) cake pan; a loaf pan; and small and medium muffin pans.

Chopping boards

I am a wooden board girl. They are more hygienic and kinder on your knives. Have different ones for meat and vegetables. Clean them regularly: scrub after each use with hot, soapy water. Rinse, dry and stand the board on its end in a dish rack to air completely. Once a week, make a paste by blending 2 tablespoons bicarbonate of soda and 1 tablespoon cold water. Smear paste over both sides of the board and allow to dry for 1 hour. Rinse and dry the board well in the sun. This will clean and deodorise is. Once dried, rub the surface with olive oil.

Food processor

Every kitchen needs a food processor. The best ones have a regular size bowl to handle big jobs like processing soup, and a small bowl for small jobs like making pesto or chopping herbs.

Fresh potted herbs

Though I am lucky enough to have a garden with the most amazing rosemary, parsley, mint and a bay tree, I still have small pots of fresh herbs on the windowsill. They are a must in every kitchen.

Good-quality foil and plastic wrap

There are many ways to save, but buying cheap, flimsy foil, baking paper and plastic wrap is not one of them. They often split, which means you use twice as much. It's a false sense of economy!

Heavy-duty kitchen scissors

These are essential to cut everything from chicken to baking paper. Never wash them in the dishwasher.

Knives

Knives are very personal. Don't purchase a set, just buy one knife at a time and the best you can afford. Eventually your set should contain a paring knife for prepping fruit and vegetables; a small serrated knife for slicing smooth skin fruit and veg like tomatoes and passionfruit; a cook's knife for all-purpose chopping; a carving knife for meat; and a large serrated knife for slicing bread and cakes.

Measuring cups and spoons

Next to knives, the most important cooks' tools are Australian Standard measuring cups and spoons. Use these for measuring dry ingredients like flour and sugar and solid ingredients like pesto and tomato paste.

Measuring jugs

It's good to have a range of these. I suggest: 2-litre Pyrex; 1-litre Pyrex; 1- and 2-cup Pyrex or plastic jugs. Use them for measuring liquids.

Microplane

These graters come in various shapes and sizes and are so versatile, finely grating everything from citrus rind, garlic, fresh ginger and chilli to parmesan cheese.

Mixing bowls

Choose various sizes, shapes and materials. Pyrex and ceramic are great for all tasks, except they will scratch from excessive use with a hand mixer over time. Metal bowls are useful, but don't use them with acidic ingredients like vinegar and citrus.

Electric mixer

If you love to bake like I do, an electric mixer (bench style) is essential.
I use both Sunbeam and Kenwood and would not part with either. A hand mixer
is also handy but not necessary if you have a bench electric mixer.

Mortar and pestle

This is another thing I would not do without. I love grinding fresh spices
like peppercorns, cinnamon, cumin and coriander. Perfect for small amounts
of pesto or curry pastes. The granite ones from Asian grocery stores are
inexpensive.

Non-slip matting

Comes in pieces or a roll. It's important to always have a piece underneath
your chopping board to prevent it from moving while you chop. It's also handy
under the electric mixer or bowls.

Oil

Variety is essential: extra virgin olive oil for dressings, all-purpose
olive oil for everything else except deep-frying (I use extra light olive oil
or peanut). Peanut oil is my choice for stir-frying.

Ovenproof frying pans

Browning food like chicken, steak, duck, fish and even sausages in a hot pan,
then placing the pan into the oven to finish off the cooking, gives the food
a lovely colour on the outside while keeping it moist. You don't need really
expensive ones. Kenwood pans are my favourite and are not expensive.

Ovenproof stovetop casserole

Though a little pricey, these cast-iron pans last a lifetime. They save time
and washing up and cook food beautifully. It's worth saving up for a good one,
so don't be tempted to buy a cheap copy.

Salt and pepper

Seasoning can be the difference between a good dish and a great dish. Sea salt flakes and freshly ground black pepper are all you find in my kitchen. The only exception to this rule is fine table salt for producing the crackling on pork rind.

Scales and timer

If you're a keen baker, a good set of electronic scales and a kitchen timer are a must.

Sieves and strainers

A conical sieve is perfect for straining soups, sauces and gravy, while a pedestal colander is essential for pasta and rice. A metal sieve is ideal for sifting, while the nylon ones should be used for fruit and sweet dishes.

Spatula

Purchase two or three (different coloured), good-quality silicon spatulas from kitchenware shops as they will last for years. Keep one for savoury and one for sweet. Don't ever put them in the dishwasher.

Spoons

I recommend a large metal spoon for folding ingredients together; a slotted spoon for removing food from oil or water; round wooden spoons for all purposes; and a flat-edged spoon for making gravy and scrambled eggs.

Whisks

A sturdy balloon whisk is essential for whipping cream and producing lump-free sauces and gravies. A coil whisk is more flexible and is great for dressings and marinades.

Wok

A well-seasoned, cheap, flat-bottom, stainless-steel wok from an Asian grocery store will last a lifetime if you cook over gas. A charn is essential to move the food around the wok quickly.

Acknowledgements

This cookbook has required dedication and commitment by a great many people who have worked tirelessly to bring it to life.

My greatest appreciation goes to Random House Australia: my publisher, Jill Brown, for her guidance and attention to detail across this entire project; the talented people in editorial and production; Annette Fitzgerald, for the stunning design; Stephanie Kistner, my editor, for just being the best; Kiren Chang, for his patience and vision for the gorgeous cover shot; Annebelle van Tongeren and Jill Love; and all the go-getters in publicity, marketing and sales — particularly my lovely publicist, Claire Rose.

The stunning food images that grace every page were shot by the master, Steve Brown: his brilliance, patience and skill are only surpassed by his kind, generous nature. Three people I feel lucky to call my friends — Kirrily, Kate and Cathie — spent long days in the kitchen cooking up the food for photography. I thank them for their outstanding work.

Thanks to my food suppliers: Mona Vale Quality Meats, Murdoch Produce and Demcos Seafood. I relied on you (and continue to rely on you) to supply the very best quality food each and every day and you never let me down.

And then there is the overwhelming generosity of Brian from Bison Homewares, Jane from Crowley and Grouch, Hannah from Robert Gordon Australia, Mimo from Sandhurst Foods, Naomi from Sunbeam Appliances, Victoria from Village Living Avalon and Laura from Liquid Ideas, who all lent me their beautiful homewares, olive oil and wine to use throughout the book.

I have been blessed by the amazing people I have worked for and with, from Margaret Fulton, Maureen Simpson, Gabriel Gate, Annette Forrest and Anneka Manning, to Mallory Hughes. In television, some special friends — Craig Sidell and Yianni Sourris, Pete Everett and the chefs, production teams, crew and makeup on *Ready Steady Cook* — have left an imprint on my heart.

Finally, thanks to my family and friends. I am lucky to have you in my life. Thank you for always being there.

Index

An Ebury Press book
Published by Random House Australia Pty Ltd
Level 3, 100 Pacific Highway, North Sydney NSW 2060
www.randomhouse.com.au

First published by Ebury Press in 2008
Text copyright © Janelle Bloom 2008
Photographs copyright © Steve Brown and Kiren Chang
The moral right of the author has been asserted.

Addresses for companies within the Random House Group can be found at
www.randomhouse.com.au/offices

National Library of Australia
Cataloguing-in-Publication Entry

Bloom, Janelle.
Fast, fresh & fabulous.

ISBN 978 1 74166 646 5 (pbk.)
Quick and easy cookery.
641.555

Cover photography by Kiren Chang
Internal photography by Steve Brown
Cover and internal design by Annette Fitzgerald
Printed and bound by Imago in Malaysia

10 9 8 7 6 5

Stockists
Bison Homewares 02 6257 7255 www.bisonhome.com
Crowley and Grouch 02 4862 1511 www.crowleyandgrouch.com
Liquid Ideas 02 9667 4211
Robert Gordon 03 5941 3144 www.robertgordonaustralia.com
Sandhurst Foods 1800 500 362 www.sandhurstfinefoods.com.au
Sunbeam Appliances 1300 881 861 www.sunbeam.com.au
Village Living 02 9918 9954